Our GRILLAHOLICS
STUFFED
BURGER PRESS
Recipe Book

OVER 99

**AMAZING RECIPES
FOR YOUR GRILLING
BBQ HAMBURGER
PATTY MAKER**

RICHARD ERWIN

Healthy Lifestyle Recipes Publishing
HLR Press
Southern California

LEGAL NOTICE

This information contained in this book is for entertainment purposes only. The content represents the opinion of the author and is based on the author's personal experience and observations. The author does not assume any liability whatsoever for the use of or inability to use any or all information contained in this book, and accepts no responsibility for any loss or damages of any kind that may be incurred by the reader as a result of actions arising from the use of the information in this book. Use this information at your own risk.

The author reserves the right to make any changes he or she deems necessary to future versions of the publication to ensure its accuracy.

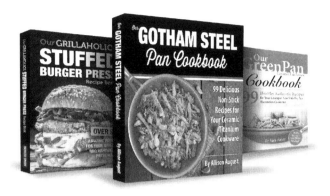

WANT FREE BOOKS?
... OF COURSE YOU DO!

Our New Books Sent To Your Email Monthly

For our current readers...if you like receiving FREE Books to add to your collection, then this is for you! This is for promoting our material to our current members so you can review our new books and give us feed back when we launch new books we are publishing! This helps us determine how we can make our books better for YOU, our audience! Just go to the url below and leave your name and email. We will send you a complimentary book about once a month. And just an FYI...on the website we've posted a few videos for you here too...

"Additional Marinades"
Yours FREE for signing up to Our List!

www.HealthyLifestyleRecipes.org/FreeBook2Review

INTRODUCTION

There's something amazingly new on the menu...and it's called "Stuffed Burgers! "**This ain't your ordinary recipe cookbook!**

This book was designed to take burger making experience to the highest level! will show you why this safe, non stick Stuffed Burger Press will be the new tool in your kitchen for years to come! This book will quickly give you the expertise you need to fully enjoy the benefits of burgers in a way that you've never seen before! Written with quick, short and easy to explain paragraphs and easy-to-understand instructions. With over 99 delicious and popular recipes at your for you to experiment with, you'll always have Great Tasting, Enormous, Mouth Watering Burgers ready to share for guests and family. In this book you will also learn: Why this book is beneficial to your kitchen and Cooking Lifestyle, All of the benefits of having this Burger Press, How to properly use this Burger Press Technology, Pro-tips to help you elevate those Burgers to another level and of course...over 99 ways to make some of the best , largest, juiciest, mouth watering, succulent burgers you've ever seen!

We show you how marinating burgers is just as important as marinating solid meats...so we've included a "Bonus Section" for those who like a good smack in the mouth flavor in every burger bite! "These mouth watering, high flavored, meat soaking marinades are amazing! A taste that you will truly love and enjoy, will give that meat the flavor it deserves!

Now..."Dive on into these Mountain High, Stuff Packed Burgers" and let see how much fun grilling and coking can be again! Impress your friends and family, and show them what they've been missing!"

If you like our book then you can **Go to Amazon where you purchased this book and <u>leave us a review</u>!** In the world of an author who writes books independently, your reviews are not only touching but important so that we know you like the material we have prepared for "YOU" our audience! So leave a nice review...we would love to see that you enjoyed our book, and we'll keep making these burgers for ya!! Enjoy, Yours Truly ~Richard Erwin

Table of Contents

legal Notice 2

Introduction 4

Chapter 1: 11

Why This Book Is Good For Your Kitchen 11
   Your One And Only! 11
   Learn How To "Stuff Em" Like A Pro! 12
   99 Problems, But A Burger Ain't One! 12
   All Hail To The Master Of Stuffing Burgers! 13
   What's In The Burger? 14

Chapter 2: 15

This Stuffed Burger Press Will Change The Life Of Your Burgers!15
   It's Easy As Pie – Or Burgers In This Case ;) 15
   Small Beef Patties Are So Last Year 16
   It Will Make Cooking Burgers Fun Again...So, Enjoy Yourself....17
   Me Like Meat, Me Strongf! 17
   Bpa Free Material – Smart, Safe And Sensible! 18

Chapter 3: 19

Benefits Of This Burger Press! 19
   "Compliments To The Chef" ...Dress That Burger To Impress! 19
   "The Endless Variety Of Burgers!" 20
   A Perfect Pressed Circle...Every Time! 21
   Togetherness 22
   "Clean As A Whistle", But Not As Loud! 23

Chapter 4: 24

There's Another Type Of Burger On The Menu 24
   Many Meats? 24
   ...And Beyond...25
   No Grill, No Problem 25
   Dinner For All! "The Possibilities Are Endless!" 25

Chapter 5: 27

How To Use You're Burger Press 27

    Easy As 1-2-3 27

    There's More To It! 28

    Presentation Matters 29

Chapter 6: 30

The "Stuff" Of Pro's 30

    Marinade That Meat 30

    Be An Inventor 31

    Be Precise 31

    Be Confident 32

    Be Humble 33

Chapter 7: 34

Putting Up The Leftovers 34

    Wrap It Up 34

    Channel Your Inner Tetris 35

    Destory The Evidence 36

    Enjoy! 37

Chapter 8: 38

Amazing Unique Recipes! 38

Chapter 9: 39

Beef Burgers: 39

    Bbq Blue Cheese Stuffed Bison Burger 39

    Tomato Basil Burger 41

    Mac & Cheese Stuffed Burger 42

    Mediterranean Style Stuffed Hamburgers 44

    Albuquerque Spicy Bison Burger 46

    Breakfast In A Bun Burger 48

    The Taste Of Korea In A Bun 49

    Fisherman Warf's Burger Stuffed With Crab 51

    Stuffed Sourdough Burger 53

    Oh My Ham And Cheese Stuffed Burger 54

Mushroom Lover Stuffed Burger 56

Stuffed Blue Cheese Burgers 58

Tarragon Infused Burger 60

Steak And Onion Marinated Burger 61

Standard American Burger 63

Portobello Covered Burgers 64

French Bread Garlic Swiss Burger 65

Short Rib And Truffle Stuffed Burger 67

Kosher Burger 69

Poultry Burgers: 71

Pollo Fiesta Burger 71

Sweet Pepper Stuffed Turkey Burger 72

Avocado Me Stuffed Turkey Burger 73

Apple Stuffed Turkey Burgers 75

The Day After Thanksgiving Burger 78

Wild West Buffalo Chicken Burger 79

Cream Cheese And Jalapeno Stuffed Burger 80

Garlic, Egg And Cheesy Ground Turkey Burger 81

Fried Zucchini Turkey Burgers 83

Vegetable Stuffed Jerk Chicken Burger 85

Chinese Infused Coleslaw Burger 87

Bacon Fried Chicken And Waffles Burger 89

Double Decker California Turkey Club Burger 91

Pork Burgers: 92

Shaved Coconut Stuffed Pork Sausage Burger 92

Ramon Noodles Spam Stuffed Burger 94

Dill Pickle Stuffed Pork Burger 95

Sweet And Spicy Pork Burger 96

Italian Pizza Pie Pork Burger 98

Cheddar Mashed Potatoes Stuffed Meatloaf Burgers 99

Guinness Stuffed Cheese Burger 101

Chinese Style Pork Burgers 102

Fish Burgers: 104

Stuffed Salmon Burger 104

Fresh Lemon Salmon Burger 106

Red Pepper Crab Cake Burger 107

California Roll Seaweed Stuffed Sushi Burger.. 109

Crab Stuffed Lobster Roll.. 111

Vegetarian/Vegan Burgers:...113

Veggie Burger With Potato 113

Love Of Mushroom Vegan Burger... 114

Squash And Sun-Dried Tomato Burger 115

Japanese Edamame And Cheese Stuffed Veggie Burger...................... 116

Arabic Chickpea Burgers 118

Healthy Burgers:..120

Miso Glazed Protein Burger 120

Super Protein Burger 122

Insane Burgers:...123

Octoberfest Burger... 123

The Sweet-Tooth Donut Burger 124

Texas Toast Grilled Cheese Stuffed Burger.. 125

Peanut Butter And Jelly Time Burger... 127

Ground Turkey Nacho Burgers 128

Luck Of The Irish Burger 129

Glazed Burgers:...130

Dijon Mustard Glazed Buffalo Burger 130

Italian Dressing Glazed Salami Burger 132

Horseradish And Dill Glazed Salmon Patties 134

Chicken Cesar Salad Glazed Burger 135

Honey Garlic Glazed Beef Burger... 136

Teriyaki Glazed Turkey Burger.. 137

Applesauce Glazed Ground Pork Burgers 138

Peanut Butter Glazed Salmon Patties.. 139

Mushroom And Balsamic Vinegar Glazed Chicken.............................. 140

Blueberry And Mint Glazed Lamb Burger 141

Wasabi Glazed Crab Cake 143

Duck Sauce Glazed Burgers 144

Swiss Bbq Glazed Burger.. 145

Plum Sauce Glazed Salmon Patties.. 146

Cubed Steak Burgers:.. 147

Bacon Wrapped Cubed Steak Burger 147

Parsley Stuffed Cubed Burger..148
French Onion Cubed Burger..149
Cabbage Wrapped Cubed Steak Burger 150
Wild Rice And Bell Pepper Stuffed Cubed Steak Burgers...................151
Burrito Wrapped Cubed Steak Burger...152

Mixed Meat Burgers: 153
Kofta Burger..153
Hot Dog Stuffed Hamburger...154
Chicken And Apple Sausage Burger..155
Ground Turkey And Sirloin Cheese Steak Burger.................................156
Ground Pork And Bison Burger...157
Fajita Burger 158
Corn Flaked Fried Zucchini And Lamb Burger......................................160
Corn Stuffed Prime Rib Burger 161
Sweet Bbq Brisket And Bratwurst Burger 162
Ground Chicken And Shrimp Burger...163
Chorizo And Black Bean Burger..164
Ground Bacon And Beef Burger..165

Fruit Stuffed Burgers: 166
Stuffed Cinnamon Apple Chicken Burger...166
Sliced Orange Pork Burger..167
Stuffed Banana Ground Beef Burger..168
Stuffed Pears Turkey Burger 169
Bing Cherry Stuffed Burger 170
Watermelon Stuffed Ground Rib Burger..171
Papaya Stuffed Spam Burger 172
Strawberry Stuffed Sausage Patty Breakfast Burger...........................173
Cheesy Scrambled Eggs Ground Bacon Burgers...................................174

"Bonus" Chapter 10: "Bonus" 175

Marinades!...175
10 Hand Selected Mouthwatering Marinades For Meats:...................175
Apple Cider Hot Mustard Garlic Marinade: 176
Cinnamon Basil Honey Marinade With Garlic 177
White Wine Jalapeño/Cayenne Marinade..178
Red Wine Sweet Cajun Marinade...179

Lemon Pepper Basil Marinade 180
Mouth Watering Mexican Style Marinade 181
Pineapple Raspberry Meat Twister Marinade 182
Italian Meat Marinating Magnifier.. 183
Mild Marinade Seafood Soaker 184
White Wine Seafood Garlic Marinade 185

DID YOU APPRECIATE THIS PUBLICATION? HERE'S WHAT YOU
DO NOW 186

A LITTLE ABOUT THE AUTHOR OF THIS BOOK.............................. 187

WANT FREE BOOKS? ... OF COURSE YOU DO! 188
Our New Books Sent To Your Email Monthly....................................... 188

Chapter 1:

WHY THIS BOOK IS GOOD FOR YOUR KITCHEN

Your One And Only!

The Burger Press market is surprisingly larger than one might think, but how can you get ahead of the game? How can you make the best burgers this side of a reality cooking show? It's simple: stuffed patties from this burger press!

The Grillaholics Stuffed Burger Press is an amazing addition to your kitchen for many reasons, but its versatility makes this such a beneficial cooking companion. There are a plethora of recipes and seemingly endless combinations of ingredients right in the palm of your hand or the pinch of your fingers.

This burger press is durable, easy to clean, and even easier to use; and because of the Grillaholics lifetime guarantee, you will be free to use this incredible product for countless meals, and your friends and families will not only be impressed...but they will fall in love with you!

Learn How To "Stuff Em" Like A Pro!

Burgers are a staple meal for backyard gatherings, cookouts, and even for just a quick and easy dinner. With that being said, there comes a point where you want your guests to stirringly proclaim, "This is amazing!" instead of calmly stating, "That was pretty good." This is the exact moment where stuffing your burgers makes the transition from *good* to *amazing* quick and easy.

We would all like the praise and recognition that comes with being a famed gourmet chef or master griller, and the average cook can accomplish that very feat with the help of the Grillaholics Stuffed Burger Press. There is the amateur way of cooking and stuffing burgers and then there is the right way! We'll show you how easy it is to transform what most like into something they can't get enough of, convinced that you've had professional training.

99 Problems, But A Burger Ain't One!

The problem with most burger eaters and cookers is that they settle for basic and sometimes bland patties. Of course it's a minor problem, but if you have the tongue and technique you might as well expand your horizons.

Imagine a world with different meats, vegetables, spices, herbs, cheeses, and everything else you can think of. That is this world! The Grillaholics Stuffed Burger Press allows you to exercise your taste buds, get creative with ingredients and their respective complements, and discover mouthwatering flavors.

You will be provided with over 99 recipes to get you started...PLUS BONUS'! Think about that: 99 and there's still so many more out there, not including your personal creations! Don't be hesitant to think outside the bun either; take your favorite and most flavorful meals and turn them into burger form! Example: Mac 'N Cheese Burger. We know. You're completely sold now.

All Hail To The Master Of Stuffing Burgers!

What does a chef like to do? Impress. Yes, a more humble answer would have been *have everyone leave the table satisfied*, but any edible substance is theoretically satisfying from the natural human need for food. There needs to be more reason for someone to kiss the cook. Is it better for boss to be impressed with your work or just satisfied? Exactly.

You never want to admit that your friends and family are your boss, unless of course the woman of the house is reading this, and we graciously accept her claim (unless she's not reading this). However, wouldn't it be nice if they all requested that you make the burgers at the next outing? With the Grillaholics Stuffed Burger Press you will learn the in's and out's of creating the perfect stuffed burger for all to enjoy!

What's In The Burger?

What's In These Burgers, you might ask...Anything you want! Anything that is edible actually, and an allergy check is also recommended before diving into the ingredient pool; we can't be giving people too much freedom. However, as already stressed, the possibilities are almost endless. You don't even have to stick to just beef; or, if you're a tad on the wild side, you don't even have to stick to one meat in the same burger!

If I could read your mind I would say that you immediately thought of Bacon. Yes, Bacon can be added to almost anything, but with the Grillaholics Stuffed Burger Press it's easy to mix in everything from tomatoes to spinach, onions to jalapenos, any cheese imaginable, or everything but the kitchen sink! Oh, and there's probably a "Kitchen Sink" burger.

Chapter 2:

THIS STUFFED BURGER PRESS WILL CHANGE THE LIFE OF YOUR BURGERS!

Or Burgers In This Case ;)

The design of the Grillaholics Stuffed Burger press is so simple which means using it is even easier. It has a base for the meat and a lid that presses down. Seriously, that's just about it.

The lid has a removable cap which is brilliant for two reasons. First, if you don't want to make a stuffed burger for whatever reason then you can make a perfectly pressed patty in less than a minute. Second, for the full effect, remove the cap to have access to the cavity that creates the crater in the base of the meat, making it incredibly simple to stuff the ingredients into the burger.

With a cleanup that is as simple as cooking, you will be changing the old adage to, "Easy as burgers!"

Small Beef Patties Are So Last Year...

Your backyard isn't a State Fair, charity event, or stadium – well, for most people it's not. Therefore, you don't have to skimp on the size of your burger unless of course you were volunteered to host your family reunion and this was the one year every relative decided to come.

With the Grillaholics Stuffed Burger Press you can make thick juicy burgers; a meal within a meal! Create mountainous dishes with flavor explosions in every bite. You can alter the size, the taste, the color, and the presentation. People will be lucky to experience these gourmet takes on a classic dish. Your burgers will never be the same, and you won't have to share the good stuff with your third-cousin who you never knew before he showed up at your house.

It Will Make Cooking Burgers Fun Again...So, Enjoy Yourself

Cooking shouldn't be a stressful task, unless of course the aforementioned family reunion is upon you, or possibly your first Thanksgiving and you only have one opportunity to impress your in-laws. Those are rare and difficult occasions though, but for the most part, creating a nice meal at home can be simple and fun!

That's exactly what the Grillaholics Stuffed Burger Press does: it's easy and enjoyable to use. Because it is so simple, it allows the chef to experiment with ingredients. There are countless combinations to keep you busy in the kitchen and develop a fun and impressive hobby.

In addition, cooking is a great way to do something together as long as you're not a stubborn chef. You can get creative with your partner or even show your kids how to cook! Don't give away all your secrets though, you still want to be the best deep down.

Me Like Meat, Me Strong!

This stuffed burger press is strong and durable. We've come a long way since the first flame-broiled piece of animal, especially linguistically it would appear. However, the cooking concept of heat to meat has lasted since the beginning of man. With that in mind, the Grillaholics Stuffed Burger Press can withstand high levels of heat.

In addition, the kitchen accessory is incredibly durable which is an amazing benefit because you're going to want to use it over and over again. The press is made of heavy duty plastic that has been certified as "SOLID" professional grade quality.

With so many variations of stuffed burger recipes, the durability factor is very important because it allows you to be the best burger maker on the block, and trust me, people will be coming back for more!

BPA Free Material – Smart, Safe And Sensible!

One of the main concerns of plastic kitchenware is whether or not the accessory contains Bisphenol A, a common chemical used to harden plastics. We are still unaware of definite effects caused by the chemical, but we have come to the point where it does pose risks to one's health. It can affect the brain, gland, and behavior if someone is overexposed. With that being said, the Grillaholics Stuffed Burger Press is proud to say that the product is BPA free!

It's easy to use, safe, and very easy to clean. You can hand wash the press of simply put it in the dishwasher because it is also dishwasher safe to add to its list of great benefits. This is perfect for entertaining so you don't have to spend time in the kitchen after dinner which means more time spent with friends and family.

Chapter 3:

BENEFITS OF THIS BURGER PRESS!

"Compliments To The Chef"
...Dress That Burger To Impress!

We touched on the fact earlier that cooks love to impress their diners. There is satisfaction in praise because you know you've made people happy, especially their taste buds. Though a chef loves to impress, it's also impressive in the eyes of others that you can create a wonderful meal for all to enjoy.

When it comes to burgers, there is also a sense of competition. The grill is a respected area that men argue to be in charge of, and meat is their forte so using the Grillaholics Stuffed Burger Press puts you one step ahead of the rest.

I personally believe one of the most flattering ways a person can complement the chef is by asking for the recipe. It's natural to be hesitant to share your creations, but it's a very genuine form of praise, and if you trust the source, then feel free to give away your secret!

"The Endless Variety Of Burgers!"

The benefits of using this burger press is out of this world! You will create the most creative, mountain high, flavorful, stuffed burger creations you or your friends have ever seen! So, Put on your apron, and be a creator and artist of your new burger world! The only limit is your imagination and creativity!

A Perfect Pressed Circle...Every Time!

A burger is pretty basic to make and is noticeable to everyone. No one has ever asked, "Hey, what's this round thing on the plate?" However, how often do you see a perfectly round burger outside of a freezer at the grocery store? Rarely.

The Grillaholics Stuffed Burger press has a solid round design that allows you to create a perfect sealed circle of a STUFFED, BEEFED UP patty. One of the rare complaints people have ordering a hamburger while dining out is that the bun does not match the size or shape of the patty. This is different than the hot dog and hot dog pun packaging ratio conundrum; this is something that can be fixed with the right tool. You have that tool now!

21

I was always one to shape the patties with my hand, cupping the meat and packing it tight, but this burger press just makes it so much easier to make quality presentable burgers!

Togetherness

No need to worry about these burgers falling apart..."We got your back on that!"

Another great benefit of the Grillaholics Stuffed Burger Press design is that it compresses your patty seamlessly. Sometimes when the burgers are truly handmade, they tend to break apart after the addition of sauces or seasonings. This press holds everything into place so no flavor is lost!

Also, when everything is packed tightly then the burger cooks evenly. There are no cracks for heat to filter through and overcook one portion of the dish and leave the other close to raw. All meat and all ingredients stay together, and your family and friends still get to enjoy the insanely delicious meal together!

"Clean As A Whistle", But Not As Loud!

We've already discussed how the Grillaholics Stuffed Burger press is BPA free and is easy to clean because it is non-stick, does not create a mess, and is dishwasher safe, but one of the most overlooked benefits of the kitchenware is that it is small.

The accessory measures 4.7" x 4.6" x 2.4" and only weighs a measly 6.4 ounces! It is easy to store and move around your kitchen or out to the grill, and, if you're willing, you can transport it easily to an outdoor barbeque at a park of over to a friend's or family member's house. That way you can say, "Don't worry, I can take it from here now," when the burgers turn out unmatched to your delicious creations.

Clean and small: this product packs a lot of bang for its size and can be stored away easily if you want to keep your secret safe from the rest!

Chapter 4:

THERE'S ANOTHER TYPE OF BURGER ON THE MENU

Many Meats?

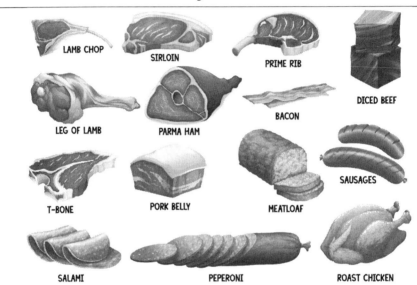

We all know that beef is the primary meat in a hamburger though it specifically says *ham* right there in the name. However, that is a different topic, but it also raises a good question. What other meats can your Burger Press shape?

All of them! Ground beef, turkey, chicken, bison, pork, anything really, even fish patties. Imagine a perfectly round crab cake. Hmm... magnificent!

This also opens up new doors for ingredient combinations, and don't forget that it's not uncommon to mix meat with meat. Ever heard of a bacon cheeseburger? Case and point. Ever heard of stuffing bacon and cheese into the burger before grilling? Because you can!

...And Beyond...

There are other alternatives to meat, more meat, and cheese to make burgers though. I know, it sounds a tad odd, but it's true and they are just as tasty!

Let's start with the stuffing. You can use spinach, tomatoes, or any other vegetable; you can enhance the flavor with chopped onions, mixed garlic, and jalapenos; and you can season with herbs and spices so they release their aromas from the inside. Mmmmmm...Delicious! ;)

Of course there is the other alternative which includes no meat at all. Portobello mushrooms, potato, corn, soy, tofu, nuts and grains, and beans can all be made into patties and shaped to perfection in this Stuffed Burger Press, again expanding the possibilities and your cooking repertoire.

No Grill, No Problem

What if it rains? What if it's too windy? What if I don't have any propane or charcoal? What if a stray or wild animal is in the backyard and I'm scared to face it? How am I supposed to cook my burgers then? All valid questions and there is one answer: Stay in the kitchen!

Three easy alternatives to the grill are broiling the patties in the oven on a broiler ban, using a griddle or pan on the stovetop, or actually steaming them in pot. Use your Grillaholics Stuffed Burger Press to create your mouthwatering masterpiece and then stay inside and use the other handy accessories in your kitchen to cook up a quick meal!

Dinner For All! "The Possibilities Are Endless!"

We live in a unique world which means there are different likes and tastes surrounding us, probably even in the same room as yourself. Therefore, this Stuffed Burger Press provides every chef with a variety of options.

Vegetarians can be happy with a meat alternative such as tofu, vegans can get excited about black bean burgers, gluten-free individuals can simply forego the bun, lactose-intolerant people can swap other cheeses with goat cheese or leave it out all together, and so on.

It's amazing the healthy and sensitive alternatives that can be made when cooking a burger. People will appreciate catering to their requests, even if they feel bad about changing the course of a meal due to their diet or allergies, but you won't mind because it's easy to do.

On the other hand, what about the children? Won't someone please think of the children? Depending on their age and appetite, you're able to decide on an appropriate size to form in your burger press, and you can make their burgers fun and exciting. Also, you can sneakily stuff in something healthy they normally would despise like beans or vegetables. Shhhhhh! I won't tell if you don't...It's a win-win if you keep it to yourself. ;)

Chapter 5:

HOW TO USE YOU'RE BURGER PRESS

Easy As 1-2-3

Being a master burger stuffer doesn't have to be hard; it's actually quite simple. You can make delicious burgers in a matter of three easy steps! We already covered the simple design of the Grillaholics Stuffed Burger Press, now let's talk quickly about how to use it. You have your ingredients ready so it's time to make some burgers!

1) Prepare your meat by dividing into sections and rounding into balls. Try not to exceed a ½ pound. Then divide each ball into a large piece and a slightly smaller one; about 60%/40% give or take.

2) Place the larger piece of meat in the Grillaholics Stuffed Burger Press. Next, remove the bottom cap from the top lid to access the cavity creator. Press down on the meat making a perfectly round and deep crater directly in the center, and then add the ingredients of your liking to the hole.

3) Take the smaller piece of meat and seal the top, trapping the ingredients within. Re-cap the top lid to create a flat base once again, cover and press down. Make sure to trim any excess meat that forms around the rim. Remove the lid and simply release the burger by pressing on the bottom tray. Transfer to a clean plate for seasoning then it's off to the grill or pan!

There's More To It!

Stuffed burgers can be a meal in their own; I believe we have covered that so far. However, there are always seemingly necessary additions that truly make this classic dish nostalgic: the bun, lettuce, tomato, onion, ketchup and/or mustard. **But what if we could liven it up a little? Good thing we can.**

There are a variety of buns on the market that can make a wonderful addition to your burger. You could try a potato bun, pretzel roll, brioche, or English muffin amongst others. There are buns with sesame seeds and other grains and flavors as well. Maybe spread a little butter on each side and toast briefly and you have the perfect complement to the patty you just created in the Grillaholics Stuffed Burger Press.

Regarding the toppings, just take the approach you did with your patty: **Do anything you want!** However, for more conventional reasons, try replacing the lettuce with spinach or kale, the tomato with something creative like eggplant or a slice of pineapple, the onion with radish slices or slivers of garlic, and the ketchup and/or mustard with barbeque sauce, mayo, or ranch!

You can be just as creative on the outside as you can on the inside. So have fun and **"Think Outside the Box!"**

Presentation Matters

When you think of burgers you don't usually affiliate gourmet with them whether it be the taste or atmosphere. Outside with the fixings atop a table and a paper plate to hold your meal is a common setting. Now that you're experienced with your Stuffed Burger Press, you might as well go all out!

Presentation matters, well sometimes, but for this section's sake it does. Let's say you made a turkey burger stuffed with feta, onions, and spinach. You placed a sliced tomato and an avocado wedge on top and stick everything between a divided buttered brioche. This deserves a classy display! Position nicely on a plate and garnish with fresh parsley or oregano. Even better yet...get a stick of rosemary and push it down the middle of the burger to hold together the masterpiece you've just created! People will rave about their dining experience, and you can stick around for the "Standing Ovation!" but don't forget to leave room for sides and to pair with your favorite drink!

Of course, as stated, presentation only sometimes matter. If you're making delicious stuffed burgers then the setting really doesn't matter.

Chapter 6:

THE "STUFF" OF PRO'S

Marinade That Meat

One of the wonderful aspects of meat is that it's very versatile. So many flavors can combine to give you a delightful taste, and even ingredients like onions and garlic are also adaptable enough to go with any meat or vegetable. It's a win-win! However, the key to juicy flavorful patties is marinating.

Marinating is a technique that comes highly-recommended. The pros do it all the time and the reason being is so the meat soaks up all the flavor, but one important aspect to marinating is time. The longer the burger soaks, the more flavor it absorbs. Sometimes I even marinate 24-hours in advance!

With the Grillaholics Stuffed Burger Press it's easy. First make your delicious patty, marinade in your choice of sauce*, and then wrap to store or place on the grill or pan. Either way, the flavor will give your burgers an extra pop! Worcestershire sauce, honey, teriyaki, barbeque, the possibilities are endless!

*you may also marinade the meat before using the burger press.

Be An Inventor

When it comes to what sauce and spices to marinate your burgers with there are plenty of options, but Worcestershire sauce is a dependable go-to flavor enhancer. However, don't be hesitant to get creative.

Let's say you make pork patties stuffed with minced garlic and chopped onions in your Grillaholics Stuffed Burger Press. It's delectable already, but try making a mixture of chili paste (not a lot) and some pineapple juice. Splash with soy sauce to moisten and serve as a salt substitute as well, and let the burger soak in the flavor. Put a strip of bacon and a sliced pineapple on top and sandwich them between a sesame bun and you have an insanely delicious burger!

Don't forget about seasoning though. Salt and pepper are the Worcestershire sauce of the rub world, and that's not an insult, it's a compliment to their necessity. However, if we take our above burger and season the meat with some red pepper and cilantro then it definitely gives it an extra kick!

Be Precise

Precision is a great attribute of master chefs and grillers. The right combination of flavors, the right amount of ingredients, and the right amount of time all come into effect.

Some flavors don't mesh well, and any recipe you find will already avoid those mishaps, and if you're creating your own then you will find out through trial and error. Good thing the Grillaholics Stuffed Burger Press is durable enough to withstand many trials, errors, and successes! Also, be aware of the amount of ingredients you use, especially with marinades. You don't want to make it too heavy or too moist to the point where it will break apart.

In addition to ingredients and preparation, you must also be precise with your cooking. Different meats require different times on the grill or pan, and eaters have different tastes and styles they prefer. Here is a small table for reference:

DONENESS	BEEF & LAMB	POULTRY	PORK
Rare (Cool Red Center)	125 Degrees	n/a	n/a
Medium Rare (Warm Red Center)	130-135 Degrees	n/a	145 Degrees
Medium (Warm Pink Center)	135-140 Degrees	n/a	150 Degrees
Medium Well (Slightly Pink Center)	140-150 Degrees	n/a	155 Degrees
Well Done (Little or no Pink)	155+ Degrees	165-175 Degrees	160 Degrees

Don't undercook, don't overcook, don't make them too moist, and don't make them too dry. It takes precision to be a pro.

Be Confident

Master chefs and grillers are also incredibly confident in the kitchen. They know what tastes good and they know how to please their diners!

We spoke about the durability of the Grillaholics Stuffed Burger Press and also its easy-to-use design, and both will help you discover what works and what doesn't. If you're experimenting and you're just not sure if your creation will taste good then make one patty so you don't use up all your ingredients and split amongst friends and family members as a taste test. If it's good then you can make more in no time, and if it's bad then on to the next test!

Eventually you will master recipes and get an understanding for the basic ingredients that complement each other and which sort of meat or cuisine. Just like anything, it takes practice to become a pro.

Be Humble

You will know when you're a master, and you will know when people know you're a master. Word will spread of your burgers and skill, people will claim you're the best and beg you to open a restaurant to share your talents with everyone. Okay, we may be getting carried away right now, but the point is that you're good at making burgers.

With that being said, be humble and accept praise graciously. You can even say it's all because of the Grillaholics Stuffed Burger Press to direct the attention off you, but we all know that the you have the skill and the gadget just makes it easy for you to be pro!

Chapter 7:

PUTTING UP THE LEFTOVERS

Wrap It Up

Food storage is actually a science. Well, maybe not actually, you can't major in it or anything, but the proper way to seal your leftovers and organize your refrigerator is important knowledge to have. Since you will be using your Grillaholics Stuffed Burger Press often there will be leftovers.

First, leftovers should be sealed and stored no more than two hours after you have finished cooking. Also, modern refrigerators prevent you from having to wait until your food cools; you can store it right away if you want!

It's vital that you use leak-proof containers and storage bags or quality plastic wrap, assuring that all your leftovers are airtight. If you use smaller separate containers to divide your leftovers then it will not take as long to cool which prevents contamination from certain bacteria even more, and try to remove as much air as possible before sealing.

Channel Your Inner Tetris

A clean and organized refrigerator is a happy one; it also means a happy wife from personal experience, but that is beside the point. Arranging your food products and leftovers properly is an art, but also very important. Vegetables, dairy, meat, eggs, everything has its own area!

Let's start with the shelving. You didn't know it mattered? Well, it does and there is a method behind the madness. You should store most leftovers on the upper shelves as well as drinks, dairy products, and foods that are essentially ready to consume and don't need to be cooked like vegetables and breads. The bottom shelves should be reserved for raw meats and other ingredients used for cooking that may be prone to drip. If you can't fit all your raw ingredients on the very bottom shelf, simply place a plate underneath the food just in case!

Now to the drawers and door. That's right, it's not over yet! The door should solely be used for condiments because it's actually the warmest part of the fridge so it would be wise not to place anything that requires cold temperatures or is perishable on the small shaves; things like milk and eggs for example. Drawers are also quite specific because they are meant to hold certain products depending on their respective humidity needed to stay fresh. Example: fruits and vegetables. Still be careful of meats resting above though if the drawers are on the bottom; there is still a risk of contamination. That's where the aforementioned plate comes in handy again!

Your refrigerator should remain below 40 degrees, try not to overload the fridge because it obstructs circulation of the cold air, and make sure you eat your meat leftovers within four days. You don't want your "New Burger Creations" to go to waste! Writing the date down and keeping them towards the front of the refrigerator is a handy reminder.

Destroy The Evidence

Don't worry, a crime hasn't been committed, unless of course someone stole your burger recipes and secrets which would be awful. You know you can clean your Grillaholics Stuffed Burger Press easily, but what about the rest?

There won't be much mess because the simplicity of the press, but there will be some spillage during preparation, and it is very important to clean up after the fact. You don't have to stop you're cooking to tend to the counter, but you can tidy up during and really clean after.

The extra minutes you have while your burgers are cooking can be used to wash some of your prep dishes and pick up and dispose of any stray ingredients. It will keep the kitchen tidy, and save you time after you've enjoyed your delicious meal.

Handling and cooking with raw meat has potential health risks that is why making sure the dish is cooked enough is vital, but also cleaning the juices that leaked during preparation is just as important. Use a disinfecting wipe or spray to assure that your counter is clear of bacteria such as E. coli, salmonella, and listeria. You don't want that stuff ruining a good thing. Gross!

Enjoy!

There's really only one last thing to do: Enjoy your creations! You may have gone a little overboard with your Grillaholics Stuffed Burger Press the night before, but that's not your fault; it's easy and fun to use so you're allowed to get carried away. However, if you didn't stuff yourself silly then you get to enjoy the meals the next day.

Whether you scramble the burger into your eggs in the morning, bring it to work for lunch to make everyone in the office jealous, or just relive your dinner memories from the night before it will be easy to remind yourself how good your burger is. You're a master so be proud of it!

Chapter 8:

AMAZING UNIQUE RECIPES!

When reading these recipes just remember that you are reading the views and opinions of the writer. We have also provided pretty creative Stuffed Burger Recipes for you Burger Lovers out there." So, Turn the page, "Dive - Head First" and get Grilling! :)

Chapter 9:

BEEF BURGERS:

BBQ Blue Cheese Stuffed Bison Burger

Want to try something new for dinner this week? The tanginess of the BBQ sauce and the creaminess of the cheese will make you remember this recipe.

Prep Time: 5 minutes
Cook Time: 20 Minutes
Servings: 4

INGREDIENTS:
1½ lbs. lean ground bison
Kosher Salt
Fresh Ground Pepper
½ cup BBQ Sauce
1 teaspoon garlic powder
1 cup blue cheese crumbles
4 onion slices

DIRECTIONS:
> Mix the ground bison, salt, pepper, BBQ sauce, and garlic powder into a bowl.
> Form the ground bison into eight 4 ounce balls. Create each ball into a patty by using the STUFF side of the burger press to push it down.
> Fill 1 of the patties with an onion slice and some of the blue cheese crumbles.
> Place the other patty on top of the other patty
> Use the SEAL side of the Burger Press to keep the two patties in place. Close the press firmly, which will seal the patties together. Release the press.
> Put the patties on the grill and cook for 6 minutes on each side

> Serve: Put the remaining BBQ sauce on a roll and top with lettuce and tomato.

Tomato Basil Burger

If you are a tomato lover then this is the burger for you? This fresh herb piece of meat will bring your summer to life.

Prep Time: 5 Minutes
Cook Time: 20 Minutes
Servings: 6

INGREDIENTS:

2 pounds ground chuck
5 tablespoons sun-dried tomato paste
Kosher Salt
4 ounces crumbled goat cheese
3 minced garlic cloves
3 tablespoons torn fresh basil
2 teaspoons garlic salt
12 whole sun-dried tomatoes packed in oil, chopped in half
6 slices of goat cheese
6 Kaiser Rolls
½ cup mayonnaise
24 large fresh basil leaves

DIRECTIONS:

> Mix first seven ingredients into a bowl.
> Form the ground chuck into twelve 4 ounce balls. Create each ball into a patty by using the STUFF side of the burger press to push it down.
> Fill 1 of the patties with 2 whole sun-dried tomatoes and 1 slice of goat cheeses.
> Place the other patty on top of the other patty
> Use the SEAL side of the Burger Press to keep the two patties in place. Close the press firmly, which will seal the patties together. Release the press.
> Put the patties on the grill and cook for 6 minutes on each side
> Grill over medium heat for 6 minutes on each side.
> Spread mayonnaise on a roll and garnish with 2 basil leaves on the top and bottom of the burger and then applying the bun.

Mac & Cheese Stuffed Burger

Do you remember when you used to dip French fries in your ice cream or stuff your burger with French fries? That was comfort food at its finest. Stuff your burger with mac and cheese and feel like a kid again.

Prep Time: 5 Minutes
Cook Time: 20 Minutes
Servings: 6

INGREDIENTS:
½ tbsp. butter
½ tbsp. flour
¼ cup milk
¼ tsp. salt
1/8 tsp. black pepper
½ cup grated medium Cheddar cheese
½ cup cooked macaroni noodles
2 lbs. ground chuck
Vegetable oil, for brushing on the grill rack
6 potato hamburger buns, split
6 tbsp. ketchup
6 tsp. yellow mustard

DIRECTIONS:
> **Macaroni and Cheese:** Add saucepan to the grill and melt butter and flour. Gradually pour in the milk. Remember to season with the salt and pepper. Add the shredded cheese, macaroni noodles and set aside.
>
> **Burgers:** Combine the ground chuck into a bowl with salt and pepper. Shape the mixture into 12 patties.
> Form the ground chuck into eight 12 ounce balls. Create each ball into a patty by using the STUFF side of the burger press to push it down.
> Fill 1 of the patties with macaroni and cheese, spread evenly.
> Place the other patty on top of the other patty

> Use the SEAL side of the Burger Press to keep the two patties in place. Close the press firmly, which will seal the patties together. Release the press.
> Put the patties on the grill and cook for 6 minutes on each side
> Grill over medium heat for 6 minutes on each side.
> Spread mustard and ketchup sauce on a bun and top with lettuce and tomato

Mediterranean Style Stuffed Hamburgers

Taste the Mediterranean on a bun. Yes, you heard me. This burger has the entire flavor of a Greek Salad or a Gyro, but just the way you like it, in a patty.

Prep Time: 5 Minutes
Cook Time: 15 Minutes
Servings: 6

INGREDIENTS:

2 lbs. ground beef
½ chopped tomato
½ cup crumbled feta cheese
2 tablespoons chopped red onion
2 tablespoons chopped ripe olives
1 teaspoon olive oil
¼ teaspoon dried oregano
Salt
Pepper
6 Whole Pita breads
6 lettuce leaves
6 slices tomato
1 small cucumber sliced
1/3 cup cucumber ranch salad dressing

DIRECTIONS:

›   Burgers: Combine the tomato, feta cheese, red onion and olives into a bowl.
›   Form the ground beef into twelve 4 ounce balls. Create each ball into a patty by using the STUFF side of the burger press to push it down.
›   Fill 1 of the patties with the mixture.
›   Place the other patty on top of the other patty
›   Use the SEAL side of the Burger Press to keep the two patties in place. Close the press firmly, which will seal the patties together. Release the press.
›   Put the patties on the grill and cook for 6 minutes on each side

> Serve on a pita and top with lettuce, tomato, cucumber and salad dressing.

Albuquerque Spicy Bison Burger

This burger isn't for the weak of heart. It adds a little punch to your punch and crunch to your palate; making you going back for more. Keep this recipe close because it's gonna be a hit at the table.

Prep Time: 5 Minutes
Cook Time: 20 Minutes
Servings: 3

INGREDIENTS:

1 pound ground buffalo
2 teaspoons taco seasoning
1/3 cup salsa
¼ cup guacamole
¼ cup sour cream
3 slices jalapeno jack cheese
1 canned green chili
Lettuce, shredded
1 diced tomato
French fried onion rings
3 hamburger buns

DIRECTIONS:

> Combine the ground buffalo, taco seasoning and salsa together in a bowl
> Mix the sour cream and guacamole together in a separate bowl and set to the side.
> Form the ground buffalo mixture into 6 4 ounce balls. Create each ball into a patty by using the STUFF side of the burger press to push it down.
> Fill 1 of the patties with a slice of cheese and 1 piece of ham.
> Place the other patty on top of the other patty
> Use the SEAL side of the Burger Press to keep the two patties in place. Close the press firmly, which will seal the patties together. Release the press.
> Put the patties on the grill and cook for 6 minutes on each side. Place the cheese on the burger and grill for an additional 2 minutes until cheese is melted

> Serve on a bun with green chilies, diced tomatoes, French fried onions and shredded lettuce.

Breakfast in a Bun Burger

A burger for breakfast? This burger combines all our favorites: eggs, bacon, ketchup and a patty; and all on one handy bun. You can eat this burger for breakfast, lunch or dinner.

Prep Time: 5 Minutes
Cook Time: 25 Minutes
Servings: 4

INGREDIENTS:

1 pound ground beef
Kosher salt
Ground black pepper
4 slices of Cheddar or American cheese
4 large eggs
8 bacon slices
4 buns
4 toasted sesame seed bagels

DIRECTIONS:

> Combine the ground beef and salt and pepper into a bowl.
> Form the ground beef mixture into four 4 ounce balls. Create each ball into a patty by using the STUFF side of the burger press to push it down.
> Fill 1 of the patties with a slice of cheese and 1 piece of bacon.
> Place the other patty on top of the other patty
> Use the SEAL side of the Burger Press to keep the two patties in place. Close the press firmly, which will seal the patties together. Release the press.
> Put the patties on the grill and cook for 6 minutes on each side.
> Place the eggs on the grill mat and fry for 4 minutes. Grill the bacon for 6 minutes.
> Serve on a bun with 1 piece of bacon and egg on top of the patty. Finish off with ketchup or hot sauce.

The Taste of Korea in a bun

It seems that we live in a world where combining two of something is better than the two by themselves. Just think cronuts, and bacon wrapped everything. Well, in this recipe, Korea meets the West. We take short rib meat and top it with an Asian slaw and BBQ sauce. It will make you want to revisit this dish over and over again.

Prep Time: 5 Minutes
Cook Time: 25 Minutes
Servings: 3

INGREDIENTS:
BBQ Sauce: *½ cup Soy sauce*
1 tablespoon soy sauce
¼ cup brown sugar
1 ½ tablespoon sriracha
2 cloves minced garlic
2 teaspoons ginger
2 tablespoons rice vinegar
2 teaspoons rice vinegar
2 teaspoons crushed red pepper flakes
1 tablespoon cornstarch
1 tablespoon water

Slaw: *1 cup shredded Napa cabbage*
1 shredded purple cabbage
1 sliced and seeded jalapeno
¼ sliced English cucumber
Salt

Burger: *1 pound ground short rib meat*
2 tablespoons unsalted butter
2 sesame seed hamburger buns

DIRECTIONS:
> Combine the ½ cup soy sauce, sriracha, brown sugar, ginger1 tablespoon rice vinegar and crushed red pepper flakes in a pan

and boil. Add in the cornstarch and water and cook for 10 minutes until the mixture thickens.

> Combine the jalapeno, cabbage, 1 teaspoon soy sauce, 2 teaspoons rice vinegar and remaining crushed red pepper flakes into a bowl. Combine the cucumber with the remaining rice vinegar and salt.
> Form the ground rib mixture into three 4 ounce balls. Create each ball into a patty by using the STUFF side of the burger press to push it down.
> Brush one side of the burger with BBQ Sauce
> Put the patties on the grill and cook for 6 minutes on each side.
> Serve on a bun and spread the BBQ sauce on the bun and top the patty with cucumbers and Asian slaw.

Fisherman Warf's Burger Stuffed with Crab

Who doesn't love a day at the beach? This recipe will remind you of the beach, minus the sand. Pair with a wine cooler, curl up with a book and chow down.

Prep Time: 5 Minutes
Cook Time: 20 Minutes
Servings: 6

INGREDIENTS:

2 pounds certified Angus Beef ground chuck
1 teaspoon horseradish
3 teaspoons Old Bay seasoning
1 1/3 bread crumbs
1 cup lump crabmeat
2 tablespoons chopped fresh cilantro
2 tablespoons finely chopped green onions
2 tablespoons mayonnaise
½ teaspoon Dijon mustard
1 teaspoon lemon zest
½ teaspoon ground ginger
6 buns

DIRECTIONS:

> Combine the ground beef and 2 teaspoons Old Bay Seasoning into a bowl
> Combine the cilantro, green onions, mayonnaise, lemon zest and ginger in a separate bowl.
> Combine the crabmeat, bread crumbs, cilantro, green onion, mayonnaise, mustard, lemon zest; ground ginger and remaining Old Bay Seasoning into a bowl.
> Form the ground beef mixture into twelve 4 ounce balls. Create each ball into a patty by using the STUFF side of the burger press to push it down.
> Fill 1 of the patties with a little bit of crab.
> Place the other patty on top of the other patty

› Use the SEAL side of the Burger Press to keep the two patties in place. Close the press firmly, which will seal the patties together. Release the press.
› Put the patties on the grill and cook for 6 minutes on each side.
› Serve: with spreading horse radish on the bottom bun, top with the salad mixture, the patty, Dijon mustard and the top part of the bun.

Stuffed Sourdough Burger

Who doesn't love cheese? How about feta cheese stuffed in the middle of your burger? This way you can taste the tangy richness with every bite.

Prep Time: 5 Minutes
Cook Time: 17 Minutes
Servings: 4

INGREDIENTS:

1 ½ pounds lean ground beef
¾ teaspoon plus 1/8 teaspoon salt
¼ teaspoon plus 1/8 teaspoon black pepper
2 ounces feta cheese
4 red onion slices
2 tablespoons extra virgin olive oil
4 crusty sourdough bread slices
4 teaspoons course-grained Dijon mustard
12 plum tomato slices

DIRECTIONS:

> Combine the ground beef and ¾ teaspoon salt and ¼ teaspoon pepper into a bowl.
> Form the ground beef mixture into eight 4 ounce balls. Create each ball into a patty by using the STUFF side of the burger press to push it down.
> Fill 1 of the patties with a slice of feta cheese in the center of each patty.
> Place the other patty on top of the other patty
> Use the SEAL side of the Burger Press to keep the two patties in place. Close the press firmly, which will seal the patties together. Release the press.
> Place onions in a pan and cook for 4 minutes with olive oil and the rest of the salt and pepper.
> Put the patties on the grill and cook for 6 minutes on each side.
> Serve on a bun and top with spread the Dijon mustard. Top with an onion and tomato on top of the burger patty.

Oh My Ham and Cheese Stuffed Burger

Every restaurant you go to nowadays is topping or stuffing everything with bacon. Well, try to be different. Let's stuff your burger with ham and Swiss. Believe me, you'll fall in love with it.

Prep Time: 5 Minutes
Cook Time: 10 Minutes
Servings: 4

INGREDIENTS:

1 tablespoon dried parsley
1 tablespoon Worcestershire sauce
¼ teaspoon salt
¼ teaspoon garlic powder
¼ teaspoon fresh ground pepper
1 pound ground round
½ cup shredded Swiss cheese
2 ounces thinly sliced smoked deli ham
Cooking spray
8 slices sourdough bread
4 curly leaf lettuce leaves
8 slices red onion
8 slices tomato

DIRECTIONS:

› Combine the parsley, Worcestershire sauce, salt, garlic powder, pepper and ground beef into a bowl.
› Form the ground beef mixture into eight four ounce balls. Create each ball into a patty by using the STUFF side of the burger press to push it down.
› Fill 1 of the patties with 2 teaspoons cheese and ½ ounce ham in the center of each patty.
› Place the other patty on top of the other patty
› Use the SEAL side of the Burger Press to keep the two patties in place. Close the press firmly, which will seal the patties together. Release the press.
› Place onions in a pan and cook for 4 minutes with olive oil and the rest of the salt and pepper.

> Put the patties on the grill and cook for 6 minutes on each side.
> Serve on a bun and top with 1 piece of lettuce, 2 tomato slices, and 2 onion slices.

Mushroom Lover Stuffed Burger

If you love mushrooms, then this is the burger for you. In this recipe, we cook the mushrooms right inside the burger

Prep Time: 10 Minutes
Cook Time: 40 Minutes
Servings: 8

INGREDIENTS:

1 ½ cups sliced onions
8 ounces mushrooms
1 tablespoon olive oil
2 tablespoons snipped fresh parsley
2 ½ pounds ground beef
1/3 cup Worcestershire sauce
4 minced garlic cloves
1 ½ teaspoons salt
1 teaspoon fine ground pepper
16 sliced Applewood smoked bacon
8 slices Swiss, provolone and Colby Jack Cheese
8 Kaiser Rolls toasted
Tomato slices

DIRECTIONS:

> Place the onions and mushrooms in a pan and cook for 20 minutes. Add the parsley and set to the side to cool.
> Combine the beef, Worcestershire, garlic, salt and pepper in a bowl.
> Form the ground beef mixture into sixteen 4 ounce balls. Create each ball into a patty by using the STUFF side of the burger press to push it down.
> Fill 1 of the patties with the onion mushroom filling in the center of each patty.
> Place the other patty on top of the other patty
> Use the SEAL side of the Burger Press to keep the two patties in place. Close the press firmly, which will seal the patties together. Release the press.

> Place onions in a pan and cook for 4 minutes with olive oil and the rest of the salt and pepper.
> Put the patties on the grill and cook for 6 minutes on each side.
> Serve with cheese and tomato slices.

Stuffed Blue Cheese Burgers

These burgers might seem simple, but there is nothing simple about the tanginess of the blue cheese, which pairs perfectly with the onion. It is a match made in heaven.

Prep Time: 5 Minutes
Cook Time: 40 Minutes
Servings: 4

INGREDIENTS:

1 pound lean ground beef
1/2 teaspoon Worcestershire sauce
1 teaspoon dried parsley
Salt and black pepper to taste
1 cup Roquefort or other blue cheese, crumbled
4 Kaiser Rolls, split and heated
4 slices onion, or to taste
4 lettuce leaves
4 slices tomato

DIRECTIONS

> Place the onions and mushrooms in a pan and cook for 20 minutes. Add the parsley and set to the side to cool.
> Combine the beef, Worcestershire, parsley, salt and pepper in a bowl.
> Form the ground beef mixture into four 4 ounce balls. Create each ball into a patty by using the STUFF side of the burger press to push it down.
> Fill 1 of the patties with a ¼ cup of Roquefort cheese in the center of each patty.
> Place the other patty on top of the other patty
> Use the SEAL side of the Burger Press to keep the two patties in place. Close the press firmly, which will seal the patties together. Release the press.
> Place onions in a pan and cook for 4 minutes with olive oil and the rest of the salt and pepper.
> Put the patties on the grill and cook for 6 minutes on each side.

> Serve on a heated Kaiser roll with sliced onion, lettuce, and tomato on the side.

Tarragon Infused Burger

This is a take on a really common dish. We have spiced it up infused with tarragon and parsley. It will make it a heaven of herbs.

Prep Time: 5 Minutes
Cook Time: 30 Minutes
Servings: 4

INGREDIENTS:

2 1/4 pounds lean ground beef
1 teaspoon dried tarragon
1/4 cup chopped parsley
salt and pepper to taste
3/4 cup blue cheese, crumbled

DIRECTIONS:

> Place the onions and mushrooms in a pan and cook for 20 minutes. Add the parsley and set to the side to cool.
> Combine the beef, parsley and tarragon in a bowl.
> Form the ground beef mixture into eight 4 ounce balls. Create each ball into a patty by using the STUFF side of the burger press to push it down.
> Fill 1 of the patties with 2 tbsp. of cheese in the center of each patty.
> Place the other patty on top of the other patty
> Use the SEAL side of the Burger Press to keep the two patties in place. Close the press firmly, which will seal the patties together. Release the press.
> Place onions in a pan and cook for 4 minutes with olive oil and the rest of the salt and pepper.
> Put the patties on the grill and cook for 6 minutes on each side.
> Serve with cheese and tomato slices.

Steak and Onion Marinated Burger

This recipe brings restaurant style steak to you, conveniently in a bun. Topped with mushrooms, bacon and onions, this recipe is a hit no matter how you eat it.

Prep Time: 5 Minutes
Cook Time: 10 Minutes
Servings: XX

INGREDIENTS:

¼ cup onion, chopped
1 can mushrooms, sliced
1 pound ground beef
1 pound bulk pork sausage
¼ cup Parmesan Cheese, grated
½ tsp. pepper
¼ tsp. garlic powder
2 tbsp. steak sauce
8 hamburger buns
Leaf lettuce

DIRECTIONS:

> Cook bacon for twelve minutes in a skillet. Set aside and cool. Add the onions in the bacon grease and cook until tender or 2 minutes. Crush the bacon and add it to the onion mix. Set aside.
> Combine the pork, cheese, beef, garlic powder, pepper and steak sauce in a bowl.
> Form the ground beef mixture into sixteen 4 ounce balls. Create each ball into a patty by using the STUFF side of the burger press to push it down.
> Fill 1 of the patties with the bacon mixture in the center of each patty.
> Place the other patty on top of the other patty
> Use the SEAL side of the Burger Press to keep the two patties in place. Close the press firmly, which will seal the patties together. Release the press.
> Put the patties on the grill and cook for 6 minutes on each side.

> ❯ Serve: on hamburger buns with lettuce, tomato and condiments that you desire.

Standard American Burger

Everything is better with cheese. That is the case with this simple burger recipe. The Gooeyness of the cheese really makes the ingredients shine.

Prep Time: 5 Minutes
Cook Time: 20 Minutes
Servings: 2

INGREDIENTS:

1 tablespoon finely chopped onion
1 tablespoon ketchup
1 teaspoon prepared mustard
1/4 teaspoon salt
1/8 teaspoon pepper
1/2 pound lean ground beef (90% lean)
1/4 cup finely shredded cheddar cheese
2 hamburger buns split
Lettuce leaves and tomato slices, optional

DIRECTIONS:

> Combine the onion, ketchup, mustard, salt and pepper in a bowl. Mix these ingredients with the beef.
> Form the ground beef mixture into four 4 ounce balls. Create each ball into a patty by using the STUFF side of the burger press to push it down.
> Fill 1 of the patties with a handful of cheese in the center of each patty.
> Place the other patty on top of the other patty
> Use the SEAL side of the Burger Press to keep the two patties in place. Close the press firmly, which will seal the patties together. Release the press.
> Place onions in a pan and cook for 4 minutes with olive oil and the rest of the salt and pepper.
> Put the patties on the grill and cook for 6 minutes on each side.
> Serve: on buns with lettuce and tomato if desired.

Portobello Covered Burgers

This recipe might seem like some of the other one's that you have read in this book, but I can assure you that it is different. Instead of stuffing this burger with mushrooms, we use the mushroom as the bun. Genius right?

Prep Time: 5 Minutes
Cook Time: 25 Minutes
Servings: 4

INGREDIENTS:

1 teaspoon Worcestershire sauce
1/2 teaspoon salt
1/2 teaspoon pepper
1-1/3 pounds ground beef
1/2 cup shredded cheddar cheese
5 bacon strips, cooked and crumbled
4 large Portobello mushrooms, stems removed
1 tablespoon olive oil
4 tomato slices
4 lettuce leaves

DIRECTIONS:

> Combine the beef, Worcestershire, salt and pepper in a bowl.
> Form the ground beef mixture into eight 4 ounce balls. Create each ball into a patty by using the STUFF side of the burger press to push it down.
> Put the patties on the grill and cook for 6 minutes on each side.
> Grill the mushroom caps for 3-4 minutes, turning on their sides.
> Serve: Place the mushrooms, top side down on the plate and top with tomato, lettuce and a burger. Enjoy.

French bread Garlic Swiss Burger

Want to try something new? Think out of the box a little bit? You will love the softness of the French bread paired with the ooziness of the cheese and the way that the garlic stands out.

Prep Time: 5 Minutes
Cook Time: 20 Minutes
Servings: 4

INGREDIENTS:

3 cups sliced onion
4 teaspoons olive oil
1/4 teaspoon salt
1/4 teaspoon coarsely ground pepper
1 pound lean ground beef
2 tablespoons Worcestershire sauce
1/2 teaspoon coarse ground pepper
2 cloves garlic, minced
3/4 cup shredded Swiss cheese (3 oz.)
4 3/4-inch-thick diagonally cut French bread slices
1 tablespoon olive oil

DIRECTIONS:

> Place the onions and oil in a pan and cook for 10 minutes. Add salt and pepper and set to the side to stay warm.
> Combine the beef, Worcestershire, ½ tsp. pepper and garlic in a bowl.
> Form the ground beef mixture into eight 4 ounce balls. Create each ball into a patty by using the STUFF side of the burger press to push it down.
> Fill 1 of the patties with ¼ of the cheese in the center of each patty.
> Place the other patty on top of the other patty
> Use the SEAL side of the Burger Press to keep the two patties in place. Close the press firmly, which will seal the patties together. Release the press.
> Place onions in a pan and cook for 4 minutes with olive oil and the rest of the salt and pepper.
> Put the patties on the grill and cook for 6 minutes on each side.

> ❯ Brush the bread with some olive oil and set on the grill for 3 minutes
> ❯ Serve: on a toasted piece of bread and top with the onion mix, the burger and top with another piece of bread.

Short Rib and Truffle Stuffed Burger

The tastes of this burger will seduce you and takes you to the romantic city of Paris. We have paired foie gras, with truffles and rib meat for a burger recipe that you would have never thought of in your wildest dreams.

Prep Time: 5 Minutes
Cook Time: 20 Minutes
Serving: 1

INGREDIENTS:

18 paper-thin slices preserved black truffle
¼ cup shredded red wine-braised short rib meat plus 2 tbsp. reserved braising juices
1 ounce foie gras
1 tbsp. carrot, minced
1 tbsp. celery, minced
1 tbsp. white onion, minced
6 ounces ground sirloin
4 tsp. horseradish mayonnaise
1 parmesan Kaiser roll, sliced and toasted
6 red onion strings, sliced
2 thin slices of tomato
1/3 cup packed frisee, cleaned and dried
½ tbsp. unsalted butter
6 pieces tomato confit

DIRECTIONS:

> Combine truffle slices with the short rib meat in a small bowl.
> Cook the foie gras for four minutes in a pan until browned
> Reduce the heat and add carrots, celery, white onion and salt and pepper to the pan. Cook for 1 minute.
> Add the rib mixture and braising juices and combine with the rest of the mixture in the pan.
> Form the ground rib mixture into two 4 ounce balls.
> Fill the patty with the foie gras in the center.
> Place the other patty on top of the other patty

> Use the SEAL side of the Burger Press to keep the two patties in place. Close the press firmly, which will seal the patties together. Release the press.
> Put the patties on the grill and cook for 8 minutes on each side.
> Serve: spread mayonnaise on the bottom bun, red onion, tomato slices, frisee and the burger patty. Top with butter and tomato confit. Spread the remaining mayonnaise on the top bun.

Kosher Burger

Who thought that being kosher could be so free? This recipe combines brisket, with horseradish, sour cream, potatoes and brown sugar. This is a ride that you taste buds will never want to get off of.

Prep Time: 5 Minutes
Cook Time: 20 Minutes
Servings: xx

INGREDIENTS:

1 cup sour cream
¼ cup horseradish
3 pounds ground brisket
3 tbsp. kosher salt
3 tbsp. pepper
2 tbsp. brown sugar
1 tbsp. instant espresso powder
1 pound russet potatoes
½ cup grated yellow onion
1 egg, slightly beaten
1 tbsp. flour
½ tsp. salt
½ tsp. pepper
Vegetable oil
12 slices Challah
6 kosher dill pickles

DIRECTIONS:

> Combine the sour cream and the horseradish in a small bowl.
> Form the rib mixture into six 4 ounce balls. Create each ball into a patty by using the STUFF side of the burger press to push it down.
> Fill 1 of the patties with a the onion mushroom filling in the center of each patty.
> Place the other patty on top of the other patty
> Use the SEAL side of the Burger Press to keep the two patties in place. Close the press firmly, which will seal the patties together. Release the press.

- ❯ Combine the sugar, espresso powder and water in a bowl. Set aside
- ❯ Next, grate the potatoes and rinse in cold water. Drain and place them on a clean towel. Place the potatoes in a bowl, add the onion, egg, flour, salt, and pepper.
- ❯ Place the potato mixture into the pan and fly with vegetable oil. Form the potatoes so they are the same size as the patties. Cook until golden brown.
- ❯ Place the patties on the grill and cook for 6 minutes on each side. When flipping brush the coffee glaze over the patties.
- ❯ Cook the challah slices on the grill, 2 minutes on each side.
- ❯ Slice the pickles lengthwise and pat them dry
- ❯ Serve: place each patty on a slice of challah, then a latke (potato mixture) and top with the pickle slices. Spread the cream cheese on the top slice and place on top of the burger.

POULTRY BURGERS:

Pollo Fiesta Burger

This burger will make you feel like a party in your mouth. Fresh Pico di Gallo, Jalapenos and cilantro will have you forgetting that you aren't eating a taco.

Prep Time: 5 Minutes
Cook Time: 20 Minutes
Servings: 4

INGREDIENTS:

1½ lbs. lean ground chicken
Kosher Salt
Fresh Ground Pepper
½ cup Pico Di Gallo
1 cup chopped jalapenos
1 cup shredded Mexican Blend Cheese
Fresh Cilantro

DIRECTIONS:

> Mix the ground chicken, salt, pepper and Pico di Gallo into a bowl.
> Form the ground chicken mixture into eight 4 ounce balls. Create each ball into a patty by using the STUFF side of the burger press to push it down.
> Fill 1 of the patties with Pico di Gallo, jalapenos, and cheese blend.
> Place the other patty on top of the other patty
> Use the SEAL side of the Burger Press to keep the two patties in place. Close the press firmly, which will seal the patties together. Release the press.
> Put the patties on the grill and cook for 6 minutes on each side.
> Serve: with the remaining Pico di Gallo on a roll and top with fresh cilantro.

Sweet Pepper Stuffed Turkey Burger

There is nothing wrong with going healthy. Here is a burger recipe that will satisfy your taste-buds and keep you from being guilt free.

Prep Time: 5 Minutes
Cook Time: 20 Minutes
Servings: 5

INGREDIENTS:

2 tablespoons onion soup mix
½ teaspoon garlic powder
½ teaspoon Worcestershire sauce
Salt
Pepper
1 ¼ pounds lean ground turkey
½ cup finely chopped sweet pepper
½ cup shredded part-skim mozzarella cheese
5 whole wheat hamburger buns, split

DIRECTIONS:

> Combine all ingredients, but the peppers and cheese, into a bowl. Shape the mixture into 10 patties.
> Form the ground beef mixture into ten 4 ounce balls. Create each ball into a patty by using the STUFF side of the burger press to push it down.
> Fill 1 of the patties with the sweet peppers and cheese in the center of each patty.
> Place the other patty on top of the other patty
> Use the SEAL side of the Burger Press to keep the two patties in place. Close the press firmly, which will seal the patties together. Release the press.
> Put the patties on the grill and cook for 6 minutes on each side.
> Serve with the remaining BBQ sauce on a bun and top with lettuce and tomato

Avocado Me Stuffed Turkey Burger

This recipe is packed with a ton of flavor and on a warm summer day you can choose to ditch the bun and eat on top of a bed of lettuce instead. It's your choice. Why not make it a good one?

Prep Time: 5 Minutes
Cook Time: 20 Minutes
Servings: 6

INGREDIENTS:
Burger : 2 lbs. lean ground turkey
3 green onions, finely chopped
2 cloves garlic, minced
2 tablespoons fresh parsley, finely chopped
1 tablespoon fresh sage, finely chopped
2 tablespoons Dijon mustard
2 large eggs
¼ cup almond flour
1 teaspoon salt
½ teaspoon ground white pepper
1 ½ ripe avocado, sliced

Spicy Mayo: ¼ cup paleo mayo
¼ teaspoon garlic powder
Pinch salt
½ chipotle powder
Leftover avocado slices from burgers

DIRECTIONS:
> Burgers: Combine all burger ingredients, but not avocado into a bowl.
> Cut the avocados in half and slice into three slices. Toss the remaining parts of the avocado into another bowl.
> Form the mixture into twelve 4 ounce balls. Create each ball into a patty by using the STUFF side of the burger press to push it down.
> Combine all Spicy Mayo ingredients into a bowl and smash with a fork

- Fill 1 of the patties with 1 avocado slice and some of the mayo mixture in the center of the patty.
- Place the other patty on top of the other patty
- Use the SEAL side of the Burger Press to keep the two patties in place. Close the press firmly, which will seal the patties together. Release the press.
- Put the patties on the grill and cook for 6 minutes on each side.
- Serve on a bun and top with lettuce, caramelized onions and sautéed mushrooms.

Apple Stuffed Turkey burgers

Dying to try something new? Tired of your husband requesting burgers for dinner every night? Well, here's a way to balance out the food groups and still give him what he wants. The whole family will love it.

Prep Time: 5 Minutes
Cook Time: 30 Minutes
Servings: 8

INGREDIENTS:

2 lbs. ground turkey
½ cup plain bread crumbs
1 egg
2 teaspoons spicy mustard
2 teaspoons dried parsley
Salt
Pepper
1 ½ cups apples, peeled, cored and thinly sliced
3 tablespoons butter, divided
½ teaspoon cinnamon
¼ teaspoon nutmeg
1 medium red onion, thinly sliced
1 teaspoon olive oil
1 ½ cups smoked gouda, shredded
8 hamburger buns
More cheese and topping for dressing the burgers

DIRECTIONS:

> Burgers: Combine the ground turkey, bread crumbs, egg, mustard, parsley, salt and pepper into a bowl.
> Form the ground beef mixture into eight 4 ounce balls. Create each ball into a patty by using the STUFF side of the burger press to push it down.
> Filling – Combine the apples, 2 tablespoons of butter, cinnamon and nutmeg into a saucepan. Cook on high for 5 minutes. Place the apples onto a dish.

> Next, combine the onion, remaining butter and olive oil into the pan and cook for 7 minutes.
> Fill 1 of the patties with the place the apples, onions, and cheese in the center of each patty.
> Place the other patty on top of the other patty
> Use the SEAL side of the Burger Press to keep the two patties in place. Close the press firmly, which will seal the patties together. Release the press.
> Put the patties on the grill and cook for 6 minutes on each side.
> Serve on a bun and top with all of the leftover topping

Stuffed Ostrich Burger with Bacon

Dying to try something new, but not too new? Try an ostrich burger. It's a taste of the outback with a little slice of the American pie.

Prep Time: 5 Minutes
Cook Time: 20 minutes
Servings: 6

INGREDIENTS:

1 ½ pounds ground ostrich
2 teaspoons chopped garlic
1 teaspoon grated ginger
2 teaspoons chopped chills
1 packet of chopped flat leaf parsley
Sea Salt
Fresh ground pepper
4 teaspoons onion marmalade
1 pound bacon
4 hamburger buns, toasted

DESCRIPTION:

> Combine the ground ostrich, garlic, ginger, chili's, parsley, salt and pepper together in a bowl.
> Form the ground beef mixture into six 4 ounce balls. Create each ball into a patty by using the STUFF side of the burger press to push it down.
> Fill 1 of the patties with the place the onion marmalade in the center of each patty and wrap the bacon around each patty.
> Place the other patty on top of the other patty
> Use the SEAL side of the Burger Press to keep the two patties in place. Close the press firmly, which will seal the patties together. Release the press.
> Put the patties on the grill and cook for 6 minutes on each side.
> Serve on a bun with lettuce, tomato.

The Day After Thanksgiving Burger

We all dread the thanksgiving leftovers. What are we supposed to do with them? This burger gives you the thanksgiving experience without having to slave for hours in the kitchen, and it's something you can make all year round.

Prep Time: 5 Minutes
Cook Time: 15 Minutes
Servings: 4

INGREDIENTS:

4 tablespoons butter
½ onion, chopped
¾ cups chicken stock
2 cups stuffing mix
1 teaspoon chopped fresh thyme leaves
1 pound ground turkey
1.2 teaspoon sage
2 tablespoons vegetable oil
4 brioche hamburger buns
1 cup cranberry sauce
1 cup gravy

DIRECTIONS:

> Combine the butter and onion into a pan and sauté until clear in color. Add the chicken stock and boil; stir in stuffing mix and cook until it is no longer dry.
> Combine the ground turkey, sage, thyme and salt and pepper in a bowl.
> Form the ground turkey mixture into four 4 ounce balls. Create each ball into a patty by using the STUFF side of the burger press to push it down.
> Put the patties on the grill and cook for 6 minutes on each side.
> Serve on a bun and top with all of the leftover topping
> Serve on a bun and add stuffing, cranberries and gravy on the top of each patty.

Wild West Buffalo Chicken Burger

Chicken, BBQ sauce and blue cheese dressing? What's not to like. It's like a hot wing, but in a bun. This burger will make your taste buds soar with pleasure.

Prep Time: 5 Minutes
Cook Time: 25 Minutes
Servings: 5

INGREDIENTS:

¼ cup buffalo wing sauce
2 tablespoons Kraft original Barbeque Sauce
1 pound ground chicken
1 package SHAKE 'N BAKE Extra Crispy Seasoned Coating Mix
1 egg
4 hamburger buns
4 leaf lettuce leaves
¼ cup KRAFT Blue Cheese Dressing
2 stalks celery, cut into sticks
2 carrots cut into sticks

DIRECTIONS:

› Combine the buffalo wing sauce and blue cheese dressing into a bowl.
› Combine the ground chicken, Shake 'N Bake and egg into a bowl.
› Form the ground chicken mixture into four 4 ounce balls. Create each ball into a patty by using the STUFF side of the burger press to push it down.
› Brush one side of the burger with the BBQ sauce
› Put the patties on the grill and cook for 6 minutes on each side. Spread the patty with the sauce mixture the last two minutes it is cooking.
› Serve on a bun and spread the sun and top with lettuce. Serve the celery, carrots and remaining blue cheese dressing on the side.

Cream Cheese and Jalapeno Stuffed Burger

Stuffed with cream cheese and diced jalapenos? The coolness of the cream cheese and the spice of the jalapeno is just enough to make this burger out of this world.

Prep Time: 5 Minutes
Cook Time: 40 Minutes
Servings: 3

INGREDIENTS:

1 pound ground turkey
1 diced jalapeno
3 ounces cream cheese
3 roasted, peeled and seeded jalapenos
½ cup shredded cheddar cheese
3 hamburger buns
Salt and pepper

DIRECTIONS:

> Combine diced Jalapeno with cream cheese.
> Form the ground beef mixture into three 4 ounce balls. Create each ball into a patty by using the STUFF side of the burger press to push it down.
> Fill 1 of the patties with the place the jalapeno mixture in the center of each patty.
> Place the other patty on top of the other patty
> Use the SEAL side of the Burger Press to keep the two patties in place. Close the press firmly, which will seal the patties together. Release the press.
> Place the jalapenos on the grill mat and grill for 8 minutes. Peel, slice and seed each jalapeno.
> Put the patties on the grill and cook for 6 minutes on each side.
> Serve on a bun and top with any preference of condiments.

Garlic, Egg and Cheesy Ground Turkey Burger

Garlic, eggs and cheese, how does that sound? Delicious right? Well, this burger will do just that. Take a bite and let us know how it tastes.

Prep Time: 5 Minutes
Cook Time: 5 Minutes
Servings: 2

INGREDIENTS:

1 ½ pound ground turkey
½ cup Bread crumbs
1 tbsp. Black pepper
2 tbsp. Kosher Salt
1 clove Garlic
¼ cup Steak sauce
1 Egg
6 tbsp. Pimento cheese
1 Tomato
1 Red onion
6 Green leaf lettuce leaves
6 Hamburger rolls

DIRECTIONS:

›   Combine the ground turkey, bread crumbs, black pepper, salt, garlic, steak sauce, and egg together in a large bowl, mixing thoroughly but try not to smash it all together.

›   Form the ground beef mixture into twelve 4 ounce balls. Create each ball into a patty by using the STUFF side of the burger press to push it down.

›   Fill 1 of the patties with 1 tbsp. of the pimento cheese in the center.

›   Place the other patty on top of the other patty

›   Use the SEAL side of the Burger Press to keep the two patties in place. Close the press firmly, which will seal the patties together. Release the press.

> Place the jalapenos on the grill mat and grill for 8 minutes. Peel, slice and seed each jalapeno.
> Cook the bacon in a skillet for twelve minutes
> Put the patties on the grill and cook for 6 minutes on each side.
> Serve on toasted rolls with onion, lettuce and tomato.

Fried Zucchini Turkey Burgers

There are so many different things that we top our burgers with, such as bacon, onion rings, even French fries. Who would of thought that topping the burger with friend zucchini? This not only adds a level of crunchiness to the burger that, but pairs well with all of the other ingredients in this modern day culinary marvel.

Prep Time: 5 Minutes
Cook Time: 50 Minutes
Servings: 4

INGREDIENTS:
Marinated Salad:
4 ounces feta cheese, crumbled
4 ounces canned chickpeas, drained and rinsed
2 tbsp. fresh basil, chopped
1 tbsp. fresh thyme, chopped
1 tbsp. fresh oregano, chopped
½ tsp. crushed red pepper
3 tbsp. extra virgin olive oil

Zucchini:
Olive oil
1 large zucchini, sliced into ¼ inch rounds
1 large egg
½ cup buttermilk
½ cup panko bread crumbs
¼ cup all-purpose flour
2 tbsp. parmesan cheese, grated

Burgers:
Olive oil
1 pound ground turkey
2 tbsp. panko bread crumbs
1 large egg
1 tsp. garlic powder
½ tsp. onion powder
2 tbsp. store bought olive tapenade

4 sandwich rolls, lightly toasted

DIRECTIONS:

> In a medium bowl combine the feta cheese, chickpeas, basil, thyme, oregano, crushed red pepper and salt and pepper. Lightly cover with olive oil. Set aside

> In another bowl, combine the egg and buttermilk, bread crumbs, flour, parmesan and salt and pepper.

> Dip the zucchini into the mixture, one piece at a time. Place each piece into a pan and cook for 4 minutes on each side until they are brown. Set aside.

> Combine the bread crumbs, turkey, egg, garlic powder, onion powder and salt and pepper to another bowl.

> Form the ground mixture into three four 4 ounce balls. Create each ball into a patty by using the STUFF side of the burger press to push it down.

> Add patties to the grill and cook for 8 minutes on each side.

> Serve: on the bottom of the burger roll add the olive tapenade, the burger, fried zucchini and salad, top with the top bun.

Vegetable Stuffed Jerk Chicken Burger

This recipe takes you on a trip to the Caribbean. This play on a Caribbean classic is filled with lots of flavor and packs a good punch.

Prep Time: 5 Minutes
Cook Time: 30 Minutes
Servings: 4

INGREDIENTS:

Jerk Sauce
1/2 cup Fresh lemon juice (2-3 lemons)
1/3 cup Extra-Virgin olive oil
1/3 cup Jarred jerk sauce
2 tbsp. Cajun seasoning
2 tbsp. Red pepper flakes
1 small Red bell pepper, finely chopped
1 large Jalapeño pepper, seeded and finely chopped
3 clove Garlic, minced

Vegetables
2 tbsp. Extra-Virgin olive oil
2 Carrots cut into 3-inch sticks
1 medium Zucchini, cut into 3-inch sticks
1 small Red bell pepper, cut into 3-inch strips
Kosher salt

Burgers
Canola oil, for the grill
2 lb. Ground beef chuck
Kosher salt and pepper
4 Sesame hamburger buns, split

DIRECTIONS:
Jerk Sauce:
> Combine the lemon juice, olive oil, jerk sauce, Cajun seasoning and red pepper flakes in a bowl. Whisk in the bell pepper, jalapeno and garlic. Set aside and keep cool.

Vegetables

> In a large skillet add oil, carrots, zucchini and bell peppers and cook until they are slightly softened for five minutes.
> Add ¼ cup of the jerk sauce and continue to cook the vegetables for 2 more minutes.

> Form the ground chicken mixture into four 4 ounce balls. Create each ball into a patty by using the STUFF side of the burger press to push it down.
> Fill 1 of the patties with the vegetable mixture in the center of each patty.
> Place the other patty on top of the other patty
> Use the SEAL side of the Burger Press to keep the two patties in place. Close the press firmly, which will seal the patties together. Release the press.
> Put the patties on the grill and cook for 6 minutes on each side.
> Serve on a bun and top with any preference of condiments.

Chinese Infused Coleslaw Burger

The pairing of chicken, lemongrass, soy sauce and sesame oil make this fusion of flavors so delightful. Come experience these Asian flavors in this American based burger.

Prep Time: 5 Minutes
Cook Time: 35 Minutes
Servings: 4

INGREDIENTS:

2 lbs. ground chicken
2 tablespoons soy sauce
2 tablespoons sugar
1 tablespoon toasted sesame oil
6 garlic cloves, minced
1 tablespoon minced lemongrass
1/3 cup sliced scallion
6 hamburger buns with sesame seeds
6 tablespoons butter, softened
1 tablespoon vegetable oil
6 tablespoons hoisin sauce
Sliced scallion
Sriracha Lime Mayo
3/4 cup mayonnaise
1 lime, juice and zest of
2 tablespoons sriracha chili sauce

Rainbow Sesame Slaw
2/3 cup julienned bell pepper (red, orange, yellow or any color combination)
2/3 cup julienned snow peas (strings removed)
2/3 cup julienned jicama
1 1/2 tablespoons rice wine vinegar
1 tablespoon sugar
1 tablespoon soy sauce
1 teaspoon sriracha chili sauce
1 teaspoon sesame oil
1 tablespoon toasted sesame seeds

DIRECTIONS

> Combine ground chicken, soy sauce, sugar, sesame oil, garlic, lemongrass and scallions.

> Form the ground chicken mixture into six 4 ounce balls. Create each ball into a patty by using the STUFF side of the burger press to push it down.

> Put the patties on the grill and cook for 6 minutes on each side. Brush the chicken patties with 1 tablespoon of the hoisin sauce

> Serve on a 1 tablespoon Sriracha Lime Mayo on each bottom and top bun. Place chicken on bun bottoms and top each with 1/3 cup Rainbow Sesame Slaw. Serve with any remaining slaw and mayo on the side. Garnish with scallions.

> Sriracha Lime Mayo: In small bowl, mix together mayonnaise, zest and juice of lime and Sriracha Chile sauce. Set aside.

> Rainbow Sesame Slaw: In medium size bowl, mix together bell peppers, julienned snow peas, julienned jicama, rice wine vinegar, sugar, soy sauce, Sriracha Chile sauce, sesame oil and toasted sesame seeds.

Bacon Fried Chicken and Waffles Burger

When you hear of this Southern Classic, you think of comfort food. This recipe is a spin on that southern classic, with the waffle serving as the bun; this burger will melt in your mouth and satisfy your sweet tooth. This can be messy. It is okay to eat with your hands or fork.

Prep Time: 5 Minutes
Cook Time: 20 Minutes
Servings: 4

INGREDIENTS:

1 pound ground chicken
1 ½ cups of panko bread crumbs
1 egg
8 frozen waffles, thawed and toasted
2 tbsp. butter
Maple syrup
8 slices of bacon

DIRECTIONS

> Cook the bacon in the pan for 12 minutes until it is crispy.
> Set aside.
> Combine the ground chicken, panko and egg together.
> Form the ground chicken mixture into eight 4 ounce balls. Create each ball into a patty by using the STUFF side of the burger press to push it down.
> Fill 1 of the patties with bacon in the center of each patty.
> Place the other patty on top of the other patty
> Use the SEAL side of the Burger Press to keep the two patties in place. Close the press firmly, which will seal the patties together. Release the press.
> Place the jalapenos on the grill mat and grill for 8 minutes. Peel, slice and seed each jalapeno.
> Cook in the same pan as the bacon grease. Cook for 6 minutes on each side.

> ❯ Serve: spread butter and syrup on the waffle, add bacon and chicken patty. Spread the butter and syrup on the other waffle and add it on top to complete the burger.

Double Decker California Turkey Club Burger

Who doesn't love a patty melt or a club? This burger has both. With ground turkey, deli ham and bacon, this burger is full of protein and so much more.

Prep Time:
Cook Time:
Servings:

INGREDIENTS:
1 cup Thousand Island dressing
1 whole avocado, sliced and pitted
8 slices of bacon
1 tomato, sliced
8 pieces of spinach lettuce
2 pounds of ground turkey
8 slices of black forest ham, deli sliced
8 pieces of cheddar cheese
8 slices of sourdough, toasted and cut in half

DIRECTIONS:
> Cook the bacon in a skillet for 12 minutes until crispy.
> Form the ground turkey into eight 4 ounce balls. Create each ball into a patty by using the STUFF side of the burger press to push it down.
> Fill 1 of the patties with a slice of cheese and 1 piece of ham.
> Place the other patty on top of the other patty
> Use the SEAL side of the Burger Press to keep the two patties in place. Close the press firmly, which will seal the patties together. Release the press.
> Put the patties on the grill and cook for 6 minutes on each side
> Serve 1 piece of bread, spread with dressing, add spinach, tomato, 2 slices of bacon, burger patty, 1 more slice of bread, 1 piece of ham, and a slice of cheese, avocado and top with the last slice of bread. Repeat for the other burgers, creating four in total.

PORK BURGERS:

Shaved Coconut Stuffed Pork Sausage Burger

Coconut meat is so full of flavor and healthy for you. In this recipe we stuffed pork sausage with coconut shavings and mixed it with some fresh herbs to create an burst of island flavors in your mouth.

Prep Time: 5 Minutes
Cook Time: 20 Minutes
Servings: 4

INGREDIENTS:

1 ½ ground pork Sausage
½ cup shaved coconut
1/3 cup fresh basil leaves
1/3 cup fresh mint leaves
3 tbsp. fresh lime juice
½ small red onion, sliced
1 garlic clove, minced
Salt and pepper to taste1
4 Hawaiian Rolls, split

DIRECTIONS:

> Combine the pork sausage, basil leaves, mint leaves, lime juice, red onion and garlic cloves in a mixing bowl.
> Form the ground pork sausage into eight 4 ounce balls. Create each ball into a patty by using the STUFF side of the burger press to push it down.
> Fill 1 of the patties with 1/8 of the shaved coconut.
> Place the other patty on top of the other patty
> Use the SEAL side of the Burger Press to keep the two patties in place. Close the press firmly, which will seal the patties together. Release the press.
> Put the patties on the grill and cook for 6 minutes on each side

› Place the burgers on top of a Hawaiian roll and top with teriyaki sauce

Ramon Noodles Spam Stuffed Burger

Ramon noodles can be used in other things besides soup. This recipe combines spam, ramen noodles and all of the fixings to add a unique flavor to any burger. You would be wishing you tried this recipe soon, like when you were in college.

Prep Time:
Cook Time:
Servings:

INGREDIENTS:

1 package of ramen noodles, chicken or beef flavored
1 can spam, drained and sliced
1 pound ground pork
2 tbsp. cilantro, chopped
1 onion, chopped
1 tomato, chopped
Steamed buns, split and buttered

DIRECTIONS:

> Cook ramen noodles to package directions minus the flavor packet.
> Combine the flavor packet, cilantro, and onion with the ground pork.
> Form the ground pork into eight 4 ounce balls. Create each ball into a patty by using the STUFF side of the burger press to push it down.
> Fill 1 of the patties with a thick slice or two of spam.
> Place the other patty on top of the other patty
> Use the SEAL side of the Burger Press to keep the two patties in place. Close the press firmly, which will seal the patties together. Release the press.
> Put the patties on the grill and cook for 6 minutes on each side
> Serve: bottom part of bun, tomato slice, Ramon Noodles, patty and top bun. Can dress with Sriracha, Soy or Teriyaki Sauce.

Dill Pickle Stuffed Pork Burger

Dill Pickles have always been the perfect side to any sandwich or burger. This is why we decided to stuff this one with dill pickle slices. Here the pickle will cook into the meat and be part of the flavor, not just an addition.

Prep Time: 5 Minutes
Cook Time: 5 Minutes
Servings: 2

INGREDIENTS

1 pound ground pork
Blue cheese 2 tablespoons
Garlic cloves, chopped 2-4
Vlasic® Dill Pickle, chopped 1
2 buns, halved and grilled

DIRECTIONS:

> Form the ground pork into two 4 ounce balls. Create each ball into a patty by using the STUFF side of the burger press to push it down.
> Fill 1 of the patties with a little of the dill pickles.
> Place the other patty on top of the other patty
> Use the SEAL side of the Burger Press to keep the two patties in place. Close the press firmly, which will seal the patties together. Release the press.
> Put the patties on the grill and cook for 6 minutes on each side
> Toast your buns and add burgers to bottom buns.

Sweet and Spicy Pork Burger

This burger reminds us of traditional Hawaiian food, pork with pineapples. What makes this ground park burger is the addition of cayenne pepper for a little kick and coconut oil.   So, sit back and relax with us as we take you on a trip on the Pacific Ocean.

Prep Time: XX Minutes
Cook Time: XX Minutes
Servings: 5

INGREDIENTS:

1 ½ pounds ground pork
1 can pineapple
2 Avocados
Juice of 1/2 lime
Juice of 1/2 lemon
A pinch of cayenne pepper
Salt and pepper to taste
2 tbsp. coconut oil
1 full sweet potato, sliced

DIRECTIONS:

> Slice the pineapple, thin enough to stuff inside a burger.
> Sprinkle coconut oil on the sliced sweet potatoes and the pineapples. Place on a baking sheet and bake in the oven for 12 minutes
> Cut the avocados in half, and remove the avocado from the casing.
> Form the ground pork into eight 4 ounce balls. Create each ball into a patty by using the STUFF side of the burger press to push it down.
> Fill 1 of the patties with a slice or two of pineapple.
> Place the other patty on top of the other patty
> Use the SEAL side of the Burger Press to keep the two patties in place. Close the press firmly, which will seal the patties together. Release the press.
> Put the patties on the grill and cook for 6 minutes on each side

> Place the burgers on top of a sweet potatoes and then top with the avocado puree. You can put another sweet potato on top of the burger as a top bun.

Italian Pizza Pie Pork Burger

Pizza in a burger? Why not? This burger has all of your favorites all in one place. With the pork taking the place as Italian sausage, you can never go wrong with this burger.

Prep Time: 5 Minutes
Cook Time: 20 Minutes
Servings: 2

INGREDIENTS:

1½ lbs. lean ground pork
Kosher Salt
Fresh Ground Pepper
½ cup Marinara Sauce
1 teaspoon garlic powder
½ teaspoon dried basil or oregano, crushed
4 slices Mozzarella
8 pepperoni slices

DIRECTIONS:

> Combine all ingredients, but the cheese and pepperoni.
> Form the ground pork into eight 4 ounce balls. Create each ball into a patty by using the STUFF side of the burger press to push it down.
> Fill 1 of the patties with 2 pieces of pepperoni and 1 slice of mozzarella cheese
> Place the other patty on top of the other patty
> Use the SEAL side of the Burger Press to keep the two patties in place. Close the press firmly, which will seal the patties together. Release the press.
> Put the patties on the grill and cook for 6 minutes on each side
> Put the remaining marinara sauce on a top of garlic bread and sprinkle with parmesan cheese.

Cheddar Mashed Potatoes Stuffed Meatloaf Burgers

This burger is the epitome of comfort food, but this is not your mother's weekly meatloaf. In this recipe we stuff the ground pork with cheddar mashed potatoes and top it off with Texas Toast and some ketchup. We can never forget the ketchup.

Prep Time: 5 Minutes
Cook Time: 20 Minutes
Servings: 4

INGREDIENTS:

1 package of instant cheddar mashed potatoes
½ cup button mushrooms, chopped
2 tablespoons extra virgin olive oil
½ small onion, chopped
1 small stock celery, chopped
2 cloves garlic, grated
2 tbsp. thyme, finely chopped
2 tbsp. parsley, finely chopped
2 tsp. sage, finely chopped
Salt and Pepper
Splash of sherry
2 slices white bread
1 cup milk
1 ½ pounds ground pork
1 egg, beaten
8 slices Texas Toast, toasted
Butter
Ketchup and Mustard, for topping

DIRECTIONS:

> Cook the mashed potatoes according to the instructions on the package. Cover and set aside when done.
> In a large pan, cook the mushrooms in the olive oil until brown. Then add the onion and celery and cook until soft. Add in the garlic, herbs, salt and pepper and sherry. Set aside and cool.

> In a bowl, tear the bread into pieces. Combine with milk and let soak.
> In another bowl combine the meat, soaked bread, egg and the mushroom mix.
> Form the ground pork into two 4 ounce balls. Create each ball into a patty by using the STUFF side of the burger press to push it down.
> Fill 1 of the patties with a tbsp. of cheddar mashed potatoes
> Place the other patty on top of the other patty
> Use the SEAL side of the Burger Press to keep the two patties in place. Close the press firmly, which will seal the patties together. Release the press.
> Put the patties on the grill and cook for 6 minutes on each side
> Serve on two slices of buttered Texas toast topped with Ketchup, mustard and BBQ Sauce.

Guinness Stuffed Cheese Burger

Everything is always better with beer or stout for that matter. This Irish stout burger is marinated in stout, Worcestershire sauce and shallots. It will make you feel like a regular Dubliner.

Prep Time:
Cook Time:
Servings: 4

INGREDIENTS:

1 ½ pounds ground pork
¼ cup shallots, chopped
2 tsp. Worcestershire sauce
½ tsp. salt
¼ pepper
½ cup shredded Dubliner cheese with Irish Stout
4 hamburger rolls, split
4 lettuce leaves
4 tomato slices
4 tsp. mayonnaise

DIRECTIONS:

> Combine pork, shallots, Worcestershire sauce, salt and pepper into a bowl.
> Form the ground pork into eight 4 ounce balls. Create each ball into a patty by using the STUFF side of the burger press to push it down.
> Fill 1 of the patties with 2 tbsp. of cheese.
> Place the other patty on top of the other patty
> Use the SEAL side of the Burger Press to keep the two patties in place. Close the press firmly, which will seal the patties together. Release the press.
> Put the patties on the grill and cook for 6 minutes on each side
> Serve: place 1 lettuce leaf, 1 tomato slice, and 1 burger. Spread the top roll with mayonnaise and put on top of the patty.

Chinese Style Pork Burgers

We have all heard of steamed pork buns. Well, this recipe is a play on that. Here, we combine pork fat and muscle and add carrots, ginger and red pepper flakes that will remind you of traditional Chinese Cuisine on a brioche bun.

Prep Time: 5 Minutes
Cook Time: 50 Minutes
Servings: 4

INGREDIENTS:

¾ pounds ground pork muscle
¼ pound ground pork fat
½ cup unseasoned bread crumbs
¼ cup onion, chopped
¼ cup carrots, peeled and shredded
1 raw egg
3 tbsp. fresh ginger, peeled and grated
2 tbsp. hoisin sauce
1 tbsp. sesame oil
1 tbsp. crushed red pepper flakes
6 brioche buns
1 large sweet red bell pepper

DIRECTIONS:

> Combine the burger and sausage and form 4 patties.
> Form the ground pork into four 4 ounce balls. Create each ball into a patty by using the STUFF side of the burger press to push it down.
> Slice the pepper in half and throw away the seed. Place the two halves skin down on the grill and cook for 5 minutes. Remove and set aside to cool
> Fill 1 of the patties with the sweet bell pepper
> Place the other patty on top of the other patty
> Use the SEAL side of the Burger Press to keep the two patties in place. Close the press firmly, which will seal the patties together. Release the press.
> Put the patties on the grill and cook for 6 minutes on each side

> Serve: the buns toasted, topped with lettuce and red pepper on the lettuce spread a tsp. of the hoisin sauce, sesame seeds and scallions. Place the bun on top and serve.

FISH BURGERS:

Stuffed Salmon Burger

Two always seems to be better than one nowadays. This shrimp stuffed salmon burger with a dill sauce will keep you coming back to this recipe over and over again.

Prep Time: 5 Minutes
Cook Time: 20 Minutes
Servings: 4

INGREDIENTS:

Filling:
½ cooked baby shrimp
½ teaspoon
garlic salt
1 teaspoon parsley

Patties:
1 (7 ounce) can pink salmon
1 egg
½ cup breadcrumbs
1 stalk celery, finely chopped
1 medium onion, finely chopped
1 teaspoon dill weed
1 teaspoon season salt
¼ cup mayonnaise
Cooking spray

Dill tartar sauce:
½ cup mayonnaise
2 tablespoons pickle relish
1 teaspoon dill weed

DIRECTIONS:

> Shrimp Filling: Combine shrimp, garlic and parsley in a bowl.
> Burgers: Combine the ground salmon, egg, bread crumbs, celery, onion, dill weed, season salt and mayonnaise into a bowl.

- Form the ground salmon into eight 4 ounce balls. Create each ball into a patty by using the STUFF side of the burger press to push it down.
- Fill 1 of the patties with the shrimp mixture
- Place the other patty on top of the other patty
- Use the SEAL side of the Burger Press to keep the two patties in place. Close the press firmly, which will seal the patties together. Release the press.
- Put the patties on the grill and cook for 6 minutes on each side
- Tartar Sauce : mix ingredients in a bowl.
- Grill over medium heat for 6 minutes on each side.
- Spread tartar sauce on a bun and top with lettuce and tomato.

Fresh Lemon Salmon Burger

This is a quick and easy way to eat salmon. It leaves you with the option of eating over a bun or on a bed of lettuce. You make the choice. It'll taste great either way.

Prep Time: 5 Minutes
Cook Time: 20 Minutes
Servings: 6

INGREDIENTS:
Burger:
1 (16 ounce) can salmon, drained and flaked
2 eggs
¼ cup chopped fresh parsley
2 tablespoons finely chopped onion
¼ cup Italian seasoned dry bread crumbs
2 tablespoons lemon juice
1/3 teaspoon dried basil
1 pinch red pepper flakes
1 tablespoon vegetable oil

Dressing:
2 tablespoons light mayonnaise
1 tablespoon lemon juice
1 pinch dried basil

DIRECTIONS:
> Combine all burger ingredients into a bowl.
> Form the mixture into six 4 ounce balls. Create each ball into a patty by using the STUFF side of the burger press to push it down.
> Put the patties on the grill and cook for 6 minutes on each side
> Combine all of the dressing ingredients into a small bowl.
> Serve on a bun with and spread the dressing on top for flavor.

Red Pepper Crab Cake Burger

Did you ever have a hard time making up your mind on eating seafood or a burger? Well, this is seafood in place of a burger. Don't let it fool you though, once you bite into this burger, it might become your go to every time.

Prep Time: 5 Minutes
Cook Time: 25 Minutes
Servings: 6

INGREDIENTS:
Dressing:
¼ cup mayonnaise
2 thinly sliced green onions
2 tablespoons minced drained roasted red pepper from jar
1 tablespoon fresh lemon juice
1 tablespoon ketchup
1 tablespoon hot chili sauce
1 tablespoon hot chili sauce
¼ teaspoon finely grated lemon peel

Burgers:
¼ cup mayonnaise
1 large egg
2 tablespoons ketchup
1 teaspoon finely grated lemon peel
1 teaspoon hot chili sauce
½ teaspoon coarse kosher salt
2 tablespoons minced drained roasted red pepper from jar
1 thinly sliced green onion
1 pound fresh lump crabmeat
1 ¾ cups panko
3 ciabatta rolls, halved
2 tablespoons butter
6 crisp heart of romaine lettuce leaves

DIRECTIONS:
Dressing:

> Combine all ingredients into a bowl and season with salt and pepper.

Burgers:
> Combine the first 8 ingredients into a bowl. Add in the crab meat and the panko.
> Form the crab mixture into six 4 ounce balls. Create each ball into a patty by using the STUFF side of the burger press to push it down.
> Put the patties on the grill and cook for 6 minutes on each side
> Spread butter on the rolls and place on the grill mat for 2 minutes.
> Place the burger on the grill mat and grill over medium heat for 5 minutes on each side.
> Serve on a bun and top with lettuce. Spread dressing on the burger and bun for flavor.

California Roll Seaweed Stuffed Sushi Burger

A burger wrapped in rice? This is our take on the California Roll. We have wrapped the crab cake in sushi rice, stuffed it with seaweed and topped it off with sriracha sauce for a little kick,

Prep Time: 10 Minutes
Cook Time: 45 Minutes
Servings: 2

INGREDIENTS:
Burger:
1 cup sushi rice
½ cups water
1/3 cup fish sauce
2 tbsp. sugar
¼ cup rice vinegar
¼ cup sriracha
1 pounds lump crab meat
Peanuts
Cucumber
Mint

Stuffing Mix:
1 tbsp. dried ready to use wakame (seaweed)
½ English cucumber
1 tsp. salt

Dressing for stuffing mix:
3 tbsp. rice vinegar
2 tbsp. water
1 tbsp. sugar
1 tbsp. soy sauce
½ tbsp. sesame oil

DIRECTIONS:
Stuffing mix:

> Soak wakame in water for 10 minutes to rehydrate. Drain well and transfer to a bowl.
> Cut the cucumbers into thin slices about 1/8- inches.
> Sprinkle the cucumber slices with salt and mix evenly. Squeeze out liquid and put in same bowl as wakame.
> Combine all the dressing ingredients in a small saucepan and cook over high heat until the sugar dissolves completely. Set aside to cool.
> Pour dressing over the wakame mix and mix well together. Garnish with ginger root

Burger:

> Mix the rice and water in a saucepan and bring to a boil. Reduce the heat and bring to a simmer for 20 minutes. Let it sit for 15 minutes when done cooking
> In a bowl mix some sugar, salt and a little bit of rice vinegar. Add the rice and mix all together.
> In another bowl mix the fish sauce, sugar, rice vinegar, and sriracha to create a sauce.
> Form the crab mix into four 4 ounce balls. Create each ball into a patty by using the STUFF side of the burger press to push it down. Marinade the patties in the sauce for 30 minutes.
> Place a tsp. of the stuffing mixture on top of one burger patty.
> Place the other patty on top of the other patty
> Use the SEAL side of the Burger Press to keep the two patties in place. Close the press firmly, which will seal the patties together. Release the press.
> Put the patties on the grill and cook for 6 minutes on each side
> Form the sushi rice into 4 patties that are equal size to the burgers. Put the rice patties on the grill and cook on medium heat until the rice is a nice brown color and sticks together.
> Grill the burgers 6 minutes on each side.
> Top the bottom rice patty with peanuts, followed by the burger, sliced cucumber, mint leaves and then top with the other rice patty. Repeat steps for the other burger.
> Serve any leftover stuffing on the side as salad. Eat with Saki or Japanese beer to enrich flavor.

Crab Stuffed Lobster Roll

The taste of Maine on a burger. Stuffing lobster with crab is a great way for us to celebrate this East Coast favorite. Pair it with a great wine cooler and you got yourself one memorable meal.

Prep Time:
Cook Time:
Servings:

INGREDIENTS:

1 pound lumped crab meat
4 cups cooked lobster meat, cubed
1 ¾ panko bread crumbs
1 egg, beaten
½ cup mayonnaise
¼ cup green onions, chopped
1 tbsp. celery, chopped
1 tbsp. fresh lemon juice
½ teaspoon salt
Dash hot sauce
Sliced French bread, toasted and buttered

DESCRIPTION:

> Combine the green onions, celery, lemon juice, salt and hot sauce into a bowl. Mix and toss. Set aside
> To form the burgers, combine the egg and bread crumbs into a bowl. Add the lobster meat and mix together.
> Form the lobster mixture into eight 4 ounce balls. Create each ball into a patty by using the STUFF side of the burger press to push it down.
> Fill 1 of the patties with the crab meat
> Place the other patty on top of the other patty
> Use the SEAL side of the Burger Press to keep the two patties in place. Close the press firmly, which will seal the patties together. Release the press.
> Fry in a pan for 6 minutes on each side.

> Serve: bottom of French bread add mayonnaise, place a spoonful of salad mixture, add the patty and top with the remaining bun. Serve with a wine cooler.

VEGETARIAN/VEGAN BURGERS:

Veggie Burger with Potato

This is the greatest burger for potato lovers. It is all of your favorite ingredients in a bun.

Prep Time: 5 Minutes
Cook Time: 22 Minutes
Servings: 6

INGREDIENTS:

1 cup canned black beans
1 grated carrot
½ diced medium onion
3 grated medium sized potatoes
4 chopped green onions
1 cup frozen or canned corn kernels
½ teaspoon garlic salt

DIRECTIONS:

> Drain the beans from the can and mash them.
> Combine all of the ingredients together in a bowl.
> Put the patties on the grill and cook for 3 minutes on each side
> Serve on a bun with ketchup, lettuce and tomato.

Love of Mushroom Vegan Burger

Not only is this burger vegan and gluten free, but it's also very tasty. If you love mushrooms, this is the burger for you. Top it with garlic, onions on top of a bed of lettuce and enjoy.

Prep Time: 5 Minutes
Cook Time: 15 Minutes
Servings: 6

INGREDIENTS:

1 tablespoon oil
1 diced onion
1 minced clove of garlic
3 diced green onions
½ teaspoon cumin
¾ cup diced fresh mushrooms
1 15 ounce can pinto beans
1 teaspoon parsley
Salt and pepper

DIRECTIONS:

> On a grill, sauté the garlic and onions in vegetable oil for 5 minutes, then add the cumin,
> mushrooms, and green onions and continue to cook for another five minutes. Set mixture aside.
> Mash the beans into a type of paste.
> Combine all of the ingredients together in a bowl.
> Form the mixture into six 4 ounce balls. Create each ball into a patty by using the STUFF side of the burger press to push it down.
> Place the burger on the grill mat and grill over medium heat for 3 minutes on each side.
> Serve on a bun with ketchup, lettuce and tomato.

Squash and Sun-Dried Tomato Burger

This recipe showcases squash and elevates it from a lowly side dish to a main dish. Here squash is the star of the show and once you try it, you will understand why.

Prep Time: 15 Minutes
Cook Time: 1 Hour
Servings: 4

INGREDIENTS:

1 delicata squash, halved lengthwise and seeded
1 tablespoon olive oil (optional)
salt and ground black pepper to taste
2 tablespoons butter
1 shallot, minced
1 clove garlic, minced
6 sun-dried tomatoes, chopped
1 cup bread crumbs, or more if needed
1 egg, beaten
1/4 cup grated Parmesan cheese
1/4 cup vegetable oil, or as needed

DIRECTIONS:

> Put squash on a baking sheet, sprinkle with olive oil and cook for 40 minutes at 470 degrees. Cut into cubes when it cools down.
> Cook and stir shallots and garlic in butter for 10 minutes. Stir in sun-dried tomatoes and cook for 3 more minutes.
> Add the squash to this mixture, mash and let cool down.
> Combine bread crumbs, the egg and parmesan cheese into the squash mixture.
> Form the squash mixture into four 4 ounce balls. Create each ball into a patty by using the STUFF side of the burger press to push it down.
> Fry in a nonstick pan for four to five minutes on each side.
> Serve on a whole wheat bun and choose the condiments that would work best for this burger.

Japanese Edamame and Cheese Stuffed Veggie Burger

Edamame stuffed wasabi cheese is a burger that will tease your taste buds and have you betting for more. Rich with vegetables, you will rave about its potato goodness.

Prep Time: 10 Minutes
Cook Time: 35 Minutes
Servings: 6

INGREDIENTS:
1 large sweet potato, diced
2 tbsp. extra virgin olive oil
3 large portabella mushroom caps, chopped
3 scallions, sliced
1 large zucchini squash, grated
2 large carrots, grated
1 cup rolled oats
½ cup frozen shelled edamame, thawed
2 tbsp. arrowroot powder (corn or potato starch)
2 tbsp. mustard
Juice of 1 lime
½ tsp. salt
1 0z Sincerely Brigitte Wasabi Cheese per burger
6 big tomatoes, sliced in half (serve as a bun)

DIRECTIONS:
> Cook sweet potatoes in a pot and bring to a boil, for ten minutes. Smash with fork
> Combine scallions mushrooms, carrots, zucchini and salt and cook for 8 minutes in a skillet.
> Add oats, mashed sweet potatoes, edamame powder, mustard, lime and salt to the mix. Blend it until it mixes together
> To form the burgers, combine the egg and bread crumbs into a bowl. Add the lobster meat and mix together.
> Form the mixture into twelve 4 ounce balls. Create each ball into a patty by using the STUFF side of the burger press to push it down.

> Fill 1 of the patties with a piece of cheese that has been cut up into three pieces
> Place the other patty on top of the other patty
> Use the SEAL side of the Burger Press to keep the two patties in place. Close the press firmly, which will seal the patties together. Release the press.
> Cook on the grill for 6 minutes per side.
> Serve on a wheat bun

Arabic Chickpea Burgers

This burger all different types of herbs and spices that boost up its flavor. Chickpeas stuffed in pita bread. Sounds like a great choice for an evening meal.

Prep Time: 20 Minutes
Cook Time: 1 hour
Servings: 8

INGREDIENTS:
2 tbsp. plus 1 tsp. olive oil
2 cups baby spinach
1 large yellow onion, chopped
4 cloves garlic, minced
1 ¼ cups vegetable broth
½ cup cracked freekeh
1 can chickpeas, drained, rinsed and patted dry
½ cup panko bread crumbs
¼ cup chopped parsley
¼ cup sunflower seeds, chopped
2 tbsp. fresh lemon juice
1 ½ tsp. grated lemon zest
1 ½ tsp. ground cumin
1 tsp. ground coriander
Salt and pepper
1 large egg, beaten
2 tbsp. canola oil
Small pita breads, for serving

Tzatziki:
1 cup plain yogurt
¼ cup finely shredded cucumber
1 clove garlic, minced
2 tsp. fresh minced dill
Salt and pepper

Tomato Salad:
2 tomatoes, chopped

¼ cup red onion, chopped
2 tbsp. parsley, chopped
½ of a lemon juice
Salt and pepper

DIRECTIONS:
> Cook the spinach in a skillet until wilted for 2 minutes. Remove. Let cool and then chop.
> Add the onion in the pan for 5 minutes to brown. Then add the garlic, broth and freekeh and boil. Cook for 20 minutes until the freekeh is soft.
> Combine the spinach, freekah, chickpeas, panko, parsley, sunflower seeds, lemon juice, zest, cumin and coriander to a bowl. Mash until the chickpeas are no longer chunky. Add the egg and stir. Let the mixture cool for an hour.
> To form the burgers, combine the egg and bread crumbs into a bowl. Add the lobster meat and mix together.
> Form the mixture into eight 4 ounce balls. Create each ball into a patty by using the STUFF side of the burger press to push it down.
> On the grill cook the burgers for 6 minutes on each side.
> Serve: on warm pita bread with the Tzatziki sauce and tomato salad
> Tzatziki Sauce: Combine all of the ingredients together.
> Tomato Salad: Combine all of the ingredients together.

HEALTHY BURGERS:

Miso Glazed Protein Burger

The great thing about tofu is that it tastes like what you marinate or cook it in. This miso glazed protein burger is not only healthy, but it's flavorful and the lettuce wrap adds a crunch that you would be missing if you used an ordinary bun.

Prep Time: 5 Minutes
Cook Time: 40 Minutes
Servings: 6

INGREDIENTS:

1 (14 ounce) packaged tofu
1 pound ground beef
½ cup shiitake mushrooms, sliced
2 tbsp. miso paste
1 egg, lightly beaten
1 tsp. salt
1 tsp. ground black pepper
¼ cup mirin (Japanese sweet wine)
1 teaspoon garlic paste
¼ teaspoon fresh ginger root, minced
1 tbsp. vegetable oil

DIRECTIONS:

> Press the tofu down until it is flattened. Discard the liquid and cut it into small pieces.
> Combine ground beef, tofu, mushrooms, miso, egg, salt, pepper and nutmeg in a bowl
> To form the burgers, combine the egg and bread crumbs into a bowl
> Form the mixture into six 4 ounce balls. Create each ball into a patty by using the STUFF side of the burger press to push it down.
> Stir in the sauces and the rest of the spices and put aside
> Cook the burgers on the grill for about 8 minutes on each side
> Pour the sauce on the burgers when they are almost done cooking to add the glaze

> Serve over lettuce leaves, seaweed or rice.

Super Protein Burger

This burger has three different types of protein: beef, bacon and eggs. It is packed with vegetables and a ton of flavor. This is a great burger to eat for an energy boost on a whole wheat bun or on a bed of lettuce. You decide.

Prep Time: 5 Minutes
Cook Time: 20 Minutes
Servings: 4

INGREDIENTS:

1 pound grass fed ground beef
½ white onion, minced
3 garlic cloves, minced
Salt and pepper
4 eggs
4 pieces of nitrate free bacon
1 head of lettuce
½ cup yellow mustard
1 tomato, sliced

DIRECTIONS:

> Combine the ground beef, garlic, salt, pepper and onion together.
> To form the burgers, combine the egg and bread crumbs into a bowl. Add the lobster meat and mix together.
> Form the mixture into four 4 ounce balls. Create each ball into a patty by using the STUFF side of the burger press to push it down.
> Cook the bacon in a small pan for about 12 minutes, flip often. Leave the grease in the pan. Spread the mustard on both sides of the burger and place in the pan. Cook for 6 minutes on each side.
> Wash the lettuce and remove the outer layers.
> In another pan, cook the eggs over easy.
> Serve: lettuce leaf, bacon, burger, fried egg and tomato slice. Wrap in the leaf and enjoy.

INSANE BURGERS:

Octoberfest Burger

This way you can celebrate all year round. This German inspired burger is marinated in beer and stuffed with bratwurst. It also contains cabbage and sour kraut for that unique taste, all topped off with a pretzel bun.

Prep Time: 5 Minutes
Cook Time: 40 Minutes
Servings: 6

INGREDIENTS:
1 bottle Heineken (or other type of German beer)
1 ½ pounds ground beef
1 ½ pounds bratwurst
1 ½ yellow onions, chopped
2 tsp. black pepper
1 medium head green cabbage, chopped
½ cup Lauer Kraut (not canned)
1 teaspoon salt
6 pieces of Swiss cheese
12 pieces of pretzel bread
Mustard for topping

DIRECTIONS:
> Cook the onion in a pan for 3-5 minutes. Add the chopped cabbage, sour kraut and the pepper. Cook for 15 minutes.
> Marinate the ground beef in the beer for 30 minutes
> Form the bratwurst into 6 patties. Do the same with the ground beef.
> Using the burger press put the ground beef patty at the bottom, top with a piece of Swiss cheese and then top with the bratwurst.
> Cook the patties on a grill for 6 minutes on each side.
> Create the burger: pretzel bottom bun, patty, cabbage mixture, mustard and finish with the top bun.

The Sweet-tooth Donut Burger

This is the burger to top all burgers. What better than a sweet creamy donut as a bun. The sweetness of the bun is the perfect addition to brunch with the ladies, especially when you want to provide more than just coffee and donuts.

Prep Time: 5 Minutes
Cook Time: 20 Minutes
Servings: 3

INGREDIENTS:
1 ½ pounds ground beef
3 tbsp. parsley, chopped
2 tbsp. onion, grated
House seasoning
2 tbsp. butter
3 eggs
6 slices bacon, cooked
6 glazed donuts

House seasoning:
1 cup salt
¼ cup black pepper
¼ cup garlic powder

DIRECTIONS:
> Combine the meat, parsley and onion together.
> Form the mixture into three 4 ounce balls. Create each ball into a patty by using the STUFF side of the burger press to push it down.
> Cook burgers on grill for 6 minutes on each side
> Fry bacon in a pan until cooked to your liking
> Cook eggs on a pan or grill, adding butter so they do not stick. Cook until the yolks are set.
> Place patties on donuts; top each with 2 pieces of bacon and an egg.
> Serve with coffee or juice.

Texas Toast Grilled Cheese Stuffed Burger

This is the burger of all burgers. Layered with two grilled cheese sandwiches and topped with onion rings, this burger will be a towering, mess of cheesy goodness.

Prep Time: 5 Minutes
Cook Time: 1 Hour
Servings: 4

INGREDIENTS:

4 1/3 raw beef burger patties
1 cup mushrooms, sliced
8 frozen onion rings, thawed
12 slices of cheddar cheese
4 slices of Swiss cheese
16 slices of Texas Toast
Iceberg lettuce
Secret Sauce

Secret Sauce:

½ cup Ketchup
½ cup mayonnaise
1 dill pickle, diced

DIRECTIONS:

> Prepare onion rings to package directions
> Fry bacon in a pan until it is done to your liking
> Prepare 8 grilled cheese sandwiches with one set of cheddar cheese in each
> Combine all secret sauce ingredients
> Sauté mushrooms in butter until brown
> Form the burger mixture into eight 4 ounce balls. Create each ball into a patty by using the STUFF side of the burger press to push it down.
> Grill burgers for 6 minutes on each side
> Serve: grilled cheese sandwich, burger patty, one slice of cheddar and Swiss cheese, 2 slices of bacon, sautéed mushrooms, 2 onions

rings, secret sauce, lettuce and top with remaining grilled cheese sandwich.

Peanut Butter and Jelly Time Burger

This recipe will remind you of your childhood. A burger combined with peanut butter and jelly is a comfort that you do not want to forget.

Prep Time: 5 Minutes
Cook Time: 20 Minutes
Servings: 4

INGREDIENTS:

1 pound ground beef
¼ cup dried cranberries
1 garlic cloves, minced
Salt and pepper to taste
¼ cup peanut butter
4 onion Kaiser rolls, split and toasted
¼ cup strawberry jam
¼ cup crumbled goat cheese

DIRECTIONS:

> Combine ground beef, cranberries, salt, pepper and garlic together.
> Form the mixture into four 4 ounce balls. Create each ball into a patty by using the STUFF side of the burger press to push it down.
> Cook on the grill for 6 minutes on each side
> Serve: 1 tbsp. of peanut butter on the bottom of each roll, top with the burger. Then spread 1 tbsp. of strawberry jam on the top layer of the roll. Pour 1 tbsp. of goat cheese on the top bun as well. Place the top bun on top of the patty to make complete the burger.

Ground Turkey Nacho Burgers

The Ground Turkey Nacho Burger combines both Nachos and a Burger in one sitting. The crunchiness of the potato chips makes for a delicious meal that you can still eat with your hands.

Prep Time: 5 Minutes
Cook Time: 20 Minutes
Servings: 4

INGREDIENTS:

1 cup heavy cream
2 garlic cloves, grated
2 tbsp. grated parmigiana Reggiano cheese
1 ½ pounds ground turkey
1 tbsp. Worcestershire sauce
Salt and pepper
2 tbsp. onion, grated
2 tbsp. parsley, chopped
2 tbsp. butter
2 tbsp. hot sauce
4 tortillas, heated and toasted
A bag of thick-cut potato chips
½ cup blue cheese crumbles
Chopped chives

DIRECTIONS:

> Combine cream and garlic in a pan and bring to a boil. Cook for 8 minutes while stirring in the cheese
> Combine the turkey, Worcestershire, salt, pepper, onion and parsley together.
> Form the mixture into four 4 ounce balls. Create each ball into a patty by using the STUFF side of the burger press to push it down.
> Cook on the grill for 6 minutes on each side. Pour the hot sauce and the butter onto the burgers while cooking.
> Serve: Place the burger on the bottom bun. Top with the potato chips, cream sauce, blue cheese and green onions.

Luck of the Irish Burger

St. Paddy's Day is a time for green beer, and making corned beef and cabbage. This is not the traditional corned beef and cabbage recipe. This burger recipe takes the whole idea to a brand new level, and one where you will be celebrating the luck of the Irish.

Prep Time: 5 Minutes
Cook Time: 20 Minutes
Servings:

INGREDIENTS:

½ pound ground corn beef
1 pound ground beef
¼ cup Guinness
Dash of Tabasco sauce
2 tbsp. olive oil
1 cup sauerkraut, drained
4 slices Irish cheddar cheese
4 whole wheat buns
Yellow mustard
Salt and pepper to taste

DIRECTIONS:

> Combine the corned beef, ground beef, Guinness, Tabasco and salt and pepper into a bowl. Form into four patties.
> Form the mixture into four 4 ounce balls. Create each ball into a patty by using the STUFF side of the burger press to push it down.
> Cook the burgers on the grill for 6 minutes on each side.
> Serve: Place the bottom bun, cheese, burger, sauerkraut and mustard.

GLAZED BURGERS:

Dijon Mustard Glazed Buffalo Burger

This part of the book experiments with different types of glazes that we brush onto our burgers for a richer, more intense flavor. The Dijon Mustard Glazed Buffalo Burger pairs the spiciness of the brown mustard and compliments it with the dill pickle, flavors that will have you asking why you never glazed your burgers before.

Prep Time: 5 Minutes
Cook Time: 20 Minutes
Servings: 4

INGREDIENTS:

1½ lbs. lean ground buffalo
Kosher Salt
Fresh Ground Pepper
½ cup Dijon Mustard
1 teaspoon garlic powder
4 slices of Pepper Jack Cheese
16 dill pickle chips

DIRECTIONS:

> Mix the ground buffalo, salt, pepper, ¼ Dijon Mustard sauce, and garlic powder into a bowl.
> Form the ground buffalo into eight 4 ounce balls. Create each ball into a patty by using the STUFF side of the burger press to push it down.
> Fill 1 of the patties with 4 dill pickle chips and one piece of cheese.
> Place the other patty on top of the other patty
> Use the SEAL side of the Burger Press to keep the two patties in place. Close the press firmly, which will seal the patties together. Release the press.
> Brush the patties with Dijon mustard on both sides
> Put the patties on the grill and cook for 6 minutes on each side. Put some more of the mustard on the patties before they are done cooking.

> Serve: Put the remaining Dijon mustard on a roll and top with lettuce and tomato.

Italian Dressing Glazed Salami Burger

Italian dressing is great for more than salads. This recipe stuffs salami with artichoke hearts and marinates the burger in Italian dressing. Then we finish it off with capers, tomatoes and peppercini's and use breadsticks as our bun. Enjoy.

Prep Time: 5 Minutes
Cook Time: 20 Minutes
Servings: 4

INGREDIENTS:
1½ lbs. lean ground salami
Kosher Salt
Fresh Ground Pepper
½ cup Italian dressing
1 teaspoon garlic powder
½ teaspoon dried basil or oregano, crushed
4 slices Mozzarella and Provolone
8 artichoke hearts
Capers, for taste
1 tomato, sliced
Peppercini's. Diced
4 Romaine hearts
16 breadsticks

DIRECTIONS:
> Mix the ground salami, salt, pepper, ¼ Italian dressing, and garlic powder into a bowl.
> Form the ground salami into eight 4 ounce balls. Create each ball into a patty by using the STUFF side of the burger press to push it down.
> Fill 1 of the patties with 2 artichoke hearts and one piece of provolone and mozzarella cheese.
> Place the other patty on top of the other patty
> Use the SEAL side of the Burger Press to keep the two patties in place. Close the press firmly, which will seal the patties together. Release the press.
> Brush the patties with Italian dressing on both sides

> Put the patties on the grill and cook for 6 minutes on each side. Put some more of the dressing on the patties before they are done cooking.
> Serve: Dust two breadsticks with the dressing, and top with capers, Peppercini's, the patty and a romaine heart. Top with 2 more breadsticks to finish the burger.
>

Horseradish and Dill Glazed Salmon Patties

These salmon patties are coated with horseradish and parsley for a kick that will make even those salmon dissenters love this dish. We have stuffed it with dill weed to contrast the horseradish and help calm your palate down.

Prep Time: 5 Minutes
Cook Time: 20 Minutes
Servings: 4

INGREDIENTS:

1 (16 ounce) can salmon, drained and flaked
2 eggs
¼ cup chopped fresh parsley
2 tablespoons finely chopped onion
¼ cup Italian seasoned dry bread crumbs
2 tablespoons lemon juice
1/3 teaspoon fresh dill weed
½ cup horseradish
1 pinch red pepper flakes
1 tablespoon vegetable oil

DIRECTIONS:

> Combine all burger ingredients, except the dill weed, into a bowl.
> Form the mixture into four 4 ounce balls. Create each ball into a patty by using the STUFF side of the burger press to push it down.
> Fill 1 of the patties with dill weed
> Place the other patty on top of the other patty
> Use the SEAL side of the Burger Press to keep the two patties in place. Close the press firmly, which will seal the patties together. Release the press.
> Brush the patties with horseradish before putting them on the grill
> Put the patties on the grill and cook for 6 minutes on each side
> Dab some more horseradish on the burgers before taking them off
> Serve on a honey oat wheat bun and top with the rest of the horseradish and squeeze a little lemon juice for flavor.

Chicken Cesar Salad Glazed Burger

As one of the best salads out there, we knew that Chicken Cesar Salad would make an incredible burger. It combines simple ingredients with bold flavor. We didn't want to impose on its greatness, just jazz it up a little bit. This is what we came up with.

Prep Time: 5 Minutes
Cook Time: 20 Minutes
Servings: 4

INGREDIENTS:

1½ lbs. lean ground chicken
Kosher Salt
Fresh Ground Pepper
½ cup Cesar dressing
1 bunch romaine, torn into bite size pieces
1 cup anchovies
1/3 freshly grated parmesan cheese
8 servings of ciabatta bread

DIRECTIONS:

> Mix the parmesan cheese, salt, pepper, romaine into a bowl.
> Form the ground chicken mixture into eight 4 ounce balls. Create each ball into a patty by using the STUFF side of the burger press to push it down.
> Fill 1 of the patties with the anchovies.
> Place the other patty on top of the other patty
> Use the SEAL side of the Burger Press to keep the two patties in place. Close the press firmly, which will seal the patties together. Release the press.
> Brush the patty with Cesar dressing on both sides.
> Put the patties on the grill and cook for 6 minutes on each side. Brush the patties with more dressing before they are done cooking.
> Serve: on the ciabatta bread with the rest of the dressing and the top with the salad.

Honey Garlic Glazed Beef Burger

Honey makes everything sweet and this burger is no exception. The honey glaze in the burger counteracts with the garlic and the cheese, but something about it makes it work wonders.

Prep Time: 5 Minutes
Cook Time: 20 Minutes
Servings: 5

INGREDIENTS:
4 full onions, center sliced
1 tablespoon honey
1 teaspoon garlic
1/4 teaspoon salt
 1/8 teaspoon pepper
1/2 pound lean ground beef
1/4 cup finely shredded cheddar cheese
 2 hamburger buns split
Lettuce leaves and tomato slices, optional

DIRECTIONS:
› Combine the garlic, salt and pepper in a bowl. Mix these ingredients with the beef.
› Form the ground beef mixture into four 4 ounce balls. Create each ball into a patty by using the STUFF side of the burger press to push it down.
› Fill 1 of the patties with a handful of cheese and one full onion in the center of each patty.
› Place the other patty on top of the other patty
› Use the SEAL side of the Burger Press to keep the two patties in place. Close the press firmly, which will seal the patties together. Release the press.
› Brush the patty with honey on each side
› Put the patties on the grill and cook for 6 minutes on each side. Add some more honey
› Serve on buns with lettuce and tomato if desired.

Teriyaki Glazed Turkey Burger

This tangy glaze of the teriyaki sauce pairs well with the ripeness of the pineapple. The flavor of this burger will bring a little sugar in your life.

Prep Time: 5 Minutes
Cook Time: 20 Minutes
Servings: 2

INGREDIENTS:

1 can of pineapples, rinses and drained
1 large sweet onion, sliced
½ cup teriyaki
1/4 teaspoon salt
1/8 teaspoon pepper
1/2 pound lean ground turkey
1/4 cup finely shredded Swiss cheese
2 hamburger buns split
4 bacon strips, cooked
Lettuce leaves and tomato slices, optional

DIRECTIONS:

> Combine the ground turkey, onion, salt and pepper in a bowl. Mix these ingredients with the beef.
> Form the ground turkey mixture into four 4 ounce balls. Create each ball into a patty by using the STUFF side of the burger press to push it down.
> Fill 1 of the patties with a slice of pineapple in the center of each patty.
> Place the other patty on top of the other patty
> Use the SEAL side of the Burger Press to keep the two patties in place. Close the press firmly, which will seal the patties together. Release the press.
> Brush the burger with teriyaki sauce
> Put the patties on the grill and cook for 6 minutes on each side. Add some more sauce
> Serve: on buns with lettuce and tomato, cheese and bacon slices.

Applesauce Glazed Ground Pork Burgers

Applesauce can be considered to be a Superfood. It helps your stomach when it hurts and applesauce can be used in place of sugar in some recipes. For something that is so healthy, it tastes so good. Check out how we glazed our burger with applesauce to give it a one of a kind flavor.

Prep Time: 5 Minutes
Cook Time: 20 Minutes
Servings: 4

INGREDIENTS:
1 ½ ground pork
½ cup applesauce
4 carrots, sliced
Juice of 1/2 lime
Juice of 1/2 lemon
Pinch of cayenne pepper
Salt and pepper to taste

DIRECTIONS:
> Slice the carrots, thin enough to stuff inside a burger.
> Form the ground pork into eight 4 ounce balls. Create each ball into a patty by using the STUFF side of the burger press to push it down.
> Fill 1 of the patties with a slice or two of carrot.
> Place the other patty on top of the other patty
> Use the SEAL side of the Burger Press to keep the two patties in place. Close the press firmly, which will seal the patties together. Release the press.
> Brush the burgers with applesauce on both sides before grilling
> Put the patties on the grill and cook for 6 minutes on each side
> Place the burgers on top of a Hawaiian roll and top with the rest of the applesauce.

Peanut Butter Glazed Salmon Patties

Peanuts are used in many different dishes all over the world for their healthy content. Well, we couldn't have forgotten them even if we tried. This recipe infuses radishes in side our burger, as well as glaze it with some of that nutty, peanut taste.

Prep Time: 5 Minutes
Cook Time: 20 Minutes
Servings: 4

INGREDIENTS:

1 can of salmon, drained and rinsed
½ cup of peanut butter
4 radishes, sliced
Juice of 1/2 lime1
Juice of 1/2 lemon1
Pinch of cayenne pepper
Salt and pepper to taste

DIRECTIONS:

> Slice the radishes thin enough to stuff inside a burger.
> Form the salmon into eight 4 ounce balls. Create each ball into a patty by using the STUFF side of the burger press to push it down.
> Fill 1 of the patties with a slice or two of radishes.
> Place the other patty on top of the other patty
> Use the SEAL side of the Burger Press to keep the two patties in place. Close the press firmly, which will seal the patties together. Release the press.
> Brush the burgers with peanut butter on both sides before grilling
> Put the patties on the grill and cook for 6 minutes on each side
> Place the burgers on top of a sesame seed roll and top with some strawberry jell or jam for effect.
>

Mushroom and Balsamic Vinegar Glazed Chicken

Mushrooms and balsamic vinegar are a great pair on baked chicken. So, we decided to use this same glaze on a burger. Mixing the mushrooms and the garlic will make your mouth water and have you anticipating the next buttery bite.

Prep Time: 5 Minutes
Cook Time: 20 Minutes
Servings: 4

INGREDIENTS:

1½ lbs. lean ground chicken
Kosher Salt
Fresh Ground Pepper
½ cup balsamic vinegar
1 pound fresh mushrooms, sliced
3 cloves garlic cloves, minced
8 servings of onion buns

DIRECTIONS:

> For the filling, cook the garlic in a pan for 2 minutes and then add the mushrooms and cook until tender
> Form the ground chicken into eight 4 ounce balls. Create each ball into a patty by using the STUFF side of the burger press to push it down.
> Fill 1 of the patties with the mushroom mix.
> Place the other patty on top of the other patty
> Use the SEAL side of the Burger Press to keep the two patties in place. Close the press firmly, which will seal the patties together. Release the press.
> Brush the patty with balsamic vinegar on both sides.
> Put the patties on the grill and cook for 6 minutes on each side. Brush the patties with more balsamic vinegar before they are done cooking.
> Serve: on the onion buns with the rest of the balsamic vinegar and you can melt some butter to add on the buns after you toast them.

Blueberry and Mint Glazed Lamb Burger

Lamb used to be the meal served on special occasions. Now, you can have lamb any time of the   year and bring a little sunshine and spring into your home with the taste of blueberries.

Prep Time: 5 Minutes
Cook Time: 20 Minutes
Servings: 4

INGREDIENTS:
1½ lbs. ground lamb
Kosher Salt
Fresh Ground Pepper
½ cup blueberry mint glaze
4 garlic clove, crushed
8 servings of ciabatta bread
Mint leaves, for garnish
Mint jelly, for dipping (optional)

GLAZE INGREDIENTS:
½ pint pomegranate juice
5 tbsp. blueberry preserves
1 ounce fresh mint, chopped
1 tbsp. white wine vinegar

DIRECTIONS:
> Mix all of the blueberry glaze ingredients into a pan and boil for 5 minutes. Let it cool and then strain.
> Form the ground lamb mixture into eight 4 ounce balls. Create each ball into a patty by using the STUFF side of the burger press to push it down.
> Fill 1 of the patties with 1 clove of garlic.
> Place the other patty on top of the other patty
> Use the SEAL side of the Burger Press to keep the two patties in place. Close the press firmly, which will seal the patties together. Release the press.
> Brush the patty with the blueberry mint on both sides.

> Put the patties on the grill and cook for 6 minutes on each side. Brush the patties with more dressing before they are done cooking.
> Serve: on the ciabatta bread and top with the mint leaves or mint jelly for extra flavor.

Wasabi Glazed Crab Cake

There are times when we just want something spicy. Well, this recipe aims to please. The Wasabi glazed burger will add a punch to your taste buds that will have you reaching for a glass of milk. Just remember to use the wasabi to your tolerance level when creating this burger.

Prep Time: 5 Minutes
Cook Time: 20 Minutes
Servings: 4

INGREDIENTS:

1½ pounds lump crab meat
Kosher Salt
Fresh Ground Pepper
½ cup wasabi
½ cup ginger
4 servings of hamburger buns

DIRECTIONS:

> Mix the crab cakes with the salt and pepper
> Form the crab cake mixture into eight 4 ounce balls. Create each ball into a patty by using the STUFF side of the burger press to push it down.
> Fill 1 of the patties with a quarter of the ginger.
> Place the other patty on top of the other patty
> Use the SEAL side of the Burger Press to keep the two patties in place. Close the press firmly, which will seal the patties together. Release the press.
> Brush the burger with the wasabi
> Put the patties on the grill and cook for 6 minutes on each side.
> Serve: on the bun and top with some soy sauce.

Duck Sauce Glazed Burgers

Want to create a dish that makes you stand out? The Duck Sauce Glazed Burger will. Duck is a very rich dish, but don't think that we are going to calm it down for you.

Prep Time: 5 Minutes
Cook Time: 20 Minutes
Servings: 4

INGREDIENTS:

1½ lbs. lean ground duck
Kosher Salt
Fresh Ground Pepper
½ cup duck sauce
2 full Fiji apples, halved and de-seeded
4 servings of black burger buns

DIRECTIONS:

> Mix the ground duck with the salt and pepper
> Form the ground duck mixture into eight 4 ounce balls. Create each ball into a patty by using the STUFF side of the burger press to push it down.
> Fill 1 of the patties with half of the apple.
> Place the other patty on top of the other patty
> Use the SEAL side of the Burger Press to keep the two patties in place. Close the press firmly, which will seal the patties together. Release the press.
> Brush the patty with the duck sauce on both sides
> Put the patties on the grill and cook for 6 minutes on each side.
> Serve: on the bun and top off with the rest of the duck sauce or soy sauce

Swiss BBQ Glazed Burger

Buns are so overrated. Why not wrap your burger in cheese? That is exactly what we're doing here. In this recipe we glaze the burger in BBQ Sauce and wrap it in Swiss cheese, which gives it a sweet, nutty taste and has fewer calories than a bun.

Prep Time: 5 Minutes
Cook Time: 20 Minutes
Servings: 4

INGREDIENTS:

1½ lbs. lean ground beef
Kosher Salt
Fresh Ground Pepper
2 poblano chills, sliced in half
½ cup BBQ
8 pieces of Swiss cheese

DIRECTIONS:
> Mix the ground beef with the salt and pepper
> Form the ground beef mixture into eight 4 ounce balls. Create each ball into a patty by using the STUFF side of the burger press to push it down.
> Fill 1 of the patties with half of the poblano.
> Place the other patty on top of the other patty
> Use the SEAL side of the Burger Press to keep the two patties in place. Close the press firmly, which will seal the patties together. Release the press.
> Brush the patty with BBQ Sauce
> Put the patties on the grill and cook for 6 minutes on each side.
> Serve on the Swiss cheese pieces

Plum Sauce Glazed Salmon Patties

This tangy, salty and spicy sauce adds a different element to the Salmon. Stuffing the patties with ginger will help your pallet cool off, just in time for the next bite at least.

Prep Time: 5 Minutes
Cook Time: 20 Minutes
Servings: 4

INGREDIENTS:

1 can of salmon, drained and rinsed
½ cup of fresh ginger
Kosher Salt
Fresh Ground Pepper
½ cup of plum sauce
4 servings of hamburger buns

DIRECTIONS:

> Mix the ground salmon with the salt and pepper
> Form the ground salmon mixture into eight 4 ounce balls. Create each ball into a patty by using the STUFF side of the burger press to push it down.
> Fill 1 of the patties with a quarter of the ginger
> Place the other patty on top of the other patty
> Use the SEAL side of the Burger Press to keep the two patties in place. Close the press firmly, which will seal the patties together. Release the press.
> Brush the patty with the plum sauce.
> Put the patties on the grill and cook for 6 minutes on each side. Put more plum sauce on the patties before they are done
> Serve on the bun and top with the rest of the plum sauce.

CUBED STEAK BURGERS:
Bacon Wrapped Cubed Steak Burger

Everything is always better with bacon. We feel the same way. In this dish we wrap the burger in cooked bacon strips and then stuff it with green onions. We are going to make you a believer.

Prep Time: 5 Minutes
Cook Time: 20 Minutes
Servings: 4

INGREDIENTS:

1½ lbs. cubed steak burger
Kosher Salt
Fresh Ground Pepper
8 pieces of bacon, cooked
½ cup ketchup
½ cup mustard
2 green onions, diced
4 servings of hamburger buns

DIRECTIONS:

> Mix the ground cubed steak with the salt and pepper
> Form the ground cubed steak mixture into eight 4 ounce balls. Create each ball into a patty by using the STUFF side of the burger press to push it down.
> Fill 1 of the patties with a quarter of the green onions.
> Place the other patty on top of the other patty
> Use the SEAL side of the Burger Press to keep the two patties in place. Close the press firmly, which will seal the patties together. Release the press.
> Put the patties on the grill and cook for 6 minutes on each side.
> Serve on the bun with the ketchup and mustard

Parsley Stuffed Cubed Burger

Parsley is known to brighten up the flavors in any dish. It will definitely do that in this one. The bitterness of this herb will bring out the rich goodness of the meat.

Prep Time: 5 Minutes
Cook Time: 20 Minutes
Servings: 4

INGREDIENTS:

1½ pounds cubed burger
Kosher Salt
Fresh Ground Pepper
½ cup parsley
Dijon Mustard
4 servings of hamburger buns

DIRECTIONS:

> Mix the ground cubed steak with the salt and pepper
> Form the ground cubed steak mixture into eight 4 ounce balls. Create each ball into a patty by using the STUFF side of the burger press to push it down.
> Fill 1 of the patties with some of the parsley.
> Place the other patty on top of the other patty
> Use the SEAL side of the Burger Press to keep the two patties in place. Close the press firmly, which will seal the patties together. Release the press.
> Put the patties on the grill and cook for 6 minutes on each side.
> Serve on the bun and top with Dijon mustard.

French Onion Cubed Burger

French onion soup has a very pleasant and savory taste. This taste will bring out all of the flavors in the meat. Why don't you give it a try?

Prep Time: 5 Minutes
Cook Time: 20 Minutes
Servings: 4

INGREDIENTS:

1½ lbs. cubed steak burger
2 packets of French onion soup
Kosher Salt
Fresh Ground Pepper
½ cup of shredded Swiss cheese
8 servings of sourdough bread

DIRECTIONS:

> Mix the ground cubed steak with the salt and pepper
> Form the ground cubed steak mixture into eight 4 ounce balls. Create each ball into a patty by using the STUFF side of the burger press to push it down.
> Fill 1 of the patties with part of the Swiss cheese.
> Place the other patty on top of the other patty
> Use the SEAL side of the Burger Press to keep the two patties in place. Close the press firmly, which will seal the patties together. Release the press.
> Put the patties on the grill and cook for 6 minutes on each side.
> Serve on the sourdough bread and top with some melted butter.

Cabbage Wrapped Cubed Steak Burger

Besides the fact that cabbage is a great antioxidant, like tofu, cabbage takes on the flavor of the ingredients that you are working with. So, wrapping this burger in cabbage will not harm the integrity of the meat itself.

Prep Time: 5 Minutes
Cook Time: 20 Minutes
Servings: 4

INGREDIENTS:
1½ lbs. lean ground cubed steak
Kosher Salt
Fresh Ground Pepper
½ cup sour kraut
½ cup sour cream
8 pieces of cabbage

DIRECTIONS:
> Mix the ground cubed steak with the salt and pepper
> Form the ground cube steak mixture into eight 4 ounce balls. Create each ball into a patty by using the STUFF side of the burger press to push it down.
> Fill 1 of the patties with some of the sour kraut.
> Place the other patty on top of the other patty
> Use the SEAL side of the Burger Press to keep the two patties in place. Close the press firmly, which will seal the patties together. Release the press.
> Put the patties on the grill and cook for 6 minutes on each side.
> Serve on the cabbage and top with the sour cream and put another piece of cabbage on the top.

Wild Rice and Bell Pepper Stuffed Cubed Steak Burgers

We all remember Mom's stuffed peppers recipe. Well, this is our version. Combining the cubed steak the wild rice creates a different kind of patty and the bell peppers give us those flavors that we grew up loving.

Prep Time: 5 Minutes
Cook Time: 20 Minutes
Servings: 4

INGREDIENTS:

1½ lbs. ground cubed steak
1 pound wild rice, cooked
1 orange bell pepper, diced
1 egg, beaten
Kosher Salt
Fresh Ground Pepper
4 servings of hamburger buns
1 cup of sausage gravy

DIRECTIONS:

> Mix the ground cubed steak, wild rice, salt, pepper and egg together
> Form the ground cubed steak mixture into eight 4 ounce balls. Create each ball into a patty by using the STUFF side of the burger press to push it down.
> Fill 1 of the patties with half of the orange bell peppers.
> Place the other patty on top of the other patty
> Use the SEAL side of the Burger Press to keep the two patties in place. Close the press firmly, which will seal the patties together. Release the press.
> Put the patties on the grill and cook for 6 minutes on each side.
> Serve on the bun and top with the gravy

Burrito Wrapped Cubed Steak Burger

Let me introduce the burger burrito. Not only does this burger taste like a burrito, but it's even wrapped in a tortilla. Confusing? We think you'll love it.

Prep Time: 5 Minutes
Cook Time: 20 Minutes
Servings: 4

INGREDIENTS:
½ pound ground cubed steak
Kosher Salt
Fresh Ground Pepper
1 Package Taco seasoning
2 full green onions, diced
1 full tomato, diced
1 full onion, diced
½ cup of cilantro, chopped
Sour cream
4 tortillas

DIRECTIONS:
> Mix the ground cubed steak with the salt, pepper and taco seasoning
> Form the ground cubed steak mixture into eight 4 ounce balls. Create each ball into a patty by using the STUFF side of the burger press to push it down.
> Fill 1 of the patties with ¼ of the green onion.
> Place the other patty on top of the other patty
> Use the SEAL side of the Burger Press to keep the two patties in place. Close the press firmly, which will seal the patties together. Release the press.
> Put the patties on the grill and cook for 6 minutes on each side.
> Serve in the tortilla and top with sour cream, tomato, onion and cilantro.

MIXED MEAT BURGERS:

Kofta Burger

In this section, we are introducing you to mixed meat burgers. Prepare yourself for some greatness. What better way to start off then with the kofta burger. Kofta is a type of meat that combines lamb and beef together so well, you wouldn't be able to tell the difference.

Prep Time: 5 Minutes
Cook Time: 20 Minutes
Servings: 4

INGREDIENTS:

1 ½ kotfta meat
Kosher Salt
Fresh Ground Pepper
½ cup of olives, diced
½ cup of tomatoes, diced
½ cup of cucumbers, sliced
½ cup of tzatziki sauce
4 servings of hamburger buns

DIRECTIONS:

›	Mix the ground kofta with the ground salt and pepper
›	Form the ground kofta mixture into eight 4 ounce balls. Create each ball into a patty by using the STUFF side of the burger press to push it down.
›	Fill 1 of the patties with 2 or 3 slices of cucumber.
›	Place the other patty on top of the other patty
›	Use the SEAL side of the Burger Press to keep the two patties in place. Close the press firmly, which will seal the patties together. Release the press.
›	Put the patties on the grill and cook for 6 minutes on each side.
›	Serve on the bun and top with tzatziki sauce, tomatoes, and olives.

Hot Dog Stuffed Hamburger

What's it going to be today, a hamburger or hot dog? IN this recipe, we combine a ground hot   dog patty with a regular beef hamburger patty and then stuff it with sweet relish. You can top it off any style you like.

Prep Time: 5 Minutes
Cook Time: 20 Minutes
Servings: 4

INGREDIENTS:

1 pound ground beef
1 pound ground hot dog
Kosher Salt
Fresh Ground Pepper
½ cup sweet relish
1 onion, diced
1 cup shredded cheddar cheese
4 servings of cheese hamburger buns

DIRECTIONS:

> Mix the ground beef and the ground hot dog with the salt and pepper
> Form the ground beef mixture and ground hot dog mixture into eight 4 ounce balls. Create each ball into a patty by using the STUFF side of the burger press to push it down.
> Fill 1 of the hamburger patties with half of the ¼ of the sweet relish.
> Place the hot dog patty on top of the ground beef patty
> Use the SEAL side of the Burger Press to keep the two patties in place. Close the press firmly, which will seal the patties together. Release the press.
> Put the patties on the grill and cook for 6 minutes on each side.
> Serve on the cheese bun and top with the onion and cheddar cheese

Chicken and Apple Sausage Burger

This burger makes poultry the star. Here we combine Turkey and Chicken sausage for a flavor that you won't want to miss. This is not a contest to see which one is sweeter or moister. Here   we are paring them as two fowl friends who are equally tasty and full of great flavors.

Prep Time: 5 Minutes
Cook Time: 20 Minutes
Servings: 4

INGREDIENTS:

1 pound ground turkey
1 pound ground apple smoked chicken sausage
Kosher Salt
Fresh Ground Pepper
½ cup feta cheese
½ cup fresh spinach, chopped
4 servings of hamburger buns
Ketchup, for taste
Mustard, for taste

DIRECTIONS:

Mix the ground chicken and ground turkey with the salt and pepper

› Form the ground chicken mixture and the ground turkey mixture into eight 4 ounce balls. Create each ball into a patty by using the STUFF side of the burger press to push it down.

› Fill 1 of the chicken patties with ¼ of the feta cheese and ¼ of the spinach.

› Place the other patty on top of the other patty

› Use the SEAL side of the Burger Press to keep the two patties in place. Close the press firmly, which will seal the patties together. Release the press.

› Put the patties on the grill and cook for 6 minutes on each side.

› Serve on the bun with ketchup and mustard

Ground Turkey and Sirloin Cheese Steak Burger

Who doesn't love a good cheese steak? From the texture of the meat, tossed with caramelized onions and bell peppers, and gooey cheese, this is a dish to die for. Let us introduce the ground turkey and sirloin cheese steak burger. It will totally make you think differently about cheese steaks.

Prep Time: 5 Minutes
Cook Time: 20 Minutes
Servings: 4

INGREDIENTS:
1 pound ground turkey
1 pound ground sirloin
1 white onion, diced
1 green bell pepper, diced
Kosher Salt
Fresh Ground Pepper
1 cup yellow mustard
4 servings of hamburger buns

DIRECTIONS:
> Mix the ground turkey and the ground sirloin with the salt and the pepper
> Form the ground turkey mixture and the ground sirloin into eight 4 ounce balls. Create each ball into a patty by using the STUFF side of the burger press to push it down.
> Fill 1 of the ground turkey patties with a quarter of the onion and the bell pepper.
> Place the ground sirloin patty on top of the ground turkey patty
> Use the SEAL side of the Burger Press to keep the two patties in place. Close the press firmly, which will seal the patties together. Release the press.
> Put the patties on the grill and cook for 6 minutes on each side.
> Serve on a bun and top with mustard

Ground Pork and Bison Burger

These are two different types of meat that bring different flavors. For one thing, pork is fattier than bison. But, they both provide distinct flavors that will add wonders to your palate.

Prep Time: 5 Minutes
Cook Time: 20 Minutes
Servings: 4

INGREDIENTS:
1 pound ground pork
1 pound ground bison
Kosher Salt
Fresh Ground Pepper
½ cup cinnamon
1 cup tangy BBQ sauce
½ cup of rosemary
4 servings of hamburger buns

DIRECTIONS:
> Mix the ground pork and the ground bison with the salt and pepper
> Form the ground pork mixture and the ground bison mixture into eight 4 ounce balls. Create each ball into a patty by using the STUFF side of the burger press to push it down.
> Fill 1 of the pork patties with ¼ of the rosemary.
> Place the ground bison patty on top of the ground pork patty
> Use the SEAL side of the Burger Press to keep the two patties in place. Close the press firmly, which will seal the patties together. Release the press.
> Put the patties on the grill and cook for 6 minutes on each side.
> Serve on the bun with the BBQ sauce

Fajita Burger

You're sitting in a restaurant and you can hear the sizzling skillet coming from a mile away. The server brings the skillet to your table and you have the most fun putting the whole fajita together; you put a little cheese here, a little onion and bell pepper here, and a little sour cream. Don't let us take that away from you. You can still do all of that here.

Prep Time: 5 Minutes
Cook Time: 20 Minutes
Servings: 4

INGREDIENTS:
1 pound of ground turkey
1 pound of ground pork
1 package of fajita seasoning
Kosher Salt
Fresh Ground Pepper
1 onion, diced
1 red bell pepper, diced
1 cup Mexican blend shredded cheese
Guacamole, for taste
Salsa, for taste
Sour cream, for taste
4 tostada shells

DIRECTIONS:
> Mix the ground turkey and ground pork with the salt, pepper and the fajita seasoning
> Form the ground turkey mixture and ground pork mixture into eight 4 ounce balls. Create each ball into a patty by using the STUFF side of the burger press to push it down.
> Fill 1 of the ground turkey patties with a little onion and bell pepper
> Place the ground pork patty on top of the ground turkey patty
> Use the SEAL side of the Burger Press to keep the two patties in place. Close the press firmly, which will seal the patties together. Release the press.

> Put the patties on the grill and cook for 6 minutes on each side.
> Serve on top of the tostada shell. Top with the cheese, salsa, guacamole and sour cream

Corn Flaked Fried Zucchini and Lamb Burger

Corn flakes are the best to fry with. Just crumble them up and they make the best bread crumbs. Here we paired zucchini and lamb. Topping the lamb burger with the crunchiness of the fried zucchini makes for a great romance.

Prep Time: 5 Minutes
Cook Time: 20 Minutes
Servings: 4

INGREDIENTS:

2 cups grated zucchini
1 pound of ground lamb
1 cup of corn flakes, crushed
2 eggs, beaten
½ cup of mint leaves, chopped
1 cup of mint jelly
Kosher Salt
Fresh Ground Pepper
8 servings of hamburger buns

DIRECTIONS:

> Mix the ground lamb with salt and pepper
> Combine the zucchini, eggs, and corn flakes together.
> Form the ground lamb mixture and zucchini mixture into eight 4 ounce balls. Create each ball into a patty by using the STUFF side of the burger press to push it down.
> Fill 1 of the lamb patties with the mint leaves
> Place the other patty on top of the other patty
> Use the SEAL side of the Burger Press to keep the two patties in place. Close the press firmly, which will seal the patties together. Release the press.
> Put the patties on the grill and cook for 6 minutes on each side.
> Serve on the bun and top with the mint jelly.

Corn Stuffed Prime Rib Burger

Corn is an accessory to all of our favorite comfort foods and meals. In this recipe we pair it off with ground prime rib and steak. It will make you feel like you are at the steakhouse.

Prep Time: 5 Minutes
Cook Time: 20 Minutes
Servings: 4

INGREDIENTS:

1 pound of ground prime rib
1 pound of ground ribeye steak
Kosher Salt
Fresh Ground Pepper
½ cup horseradish
2 can of corn
4 onion buns, split and toasted

DIRECTIONS:

> Mix the ground prime rib mixture and ground ribeye steak with salt and pepper
> Form the ground prime rib mixture and the ribeye steak mixture into eight 4 ounce balls. Create each ball into a patty by using the STUFF side of the burger press to push it down.
> Fill 1 of the prime rib patties with some of the corn
> Place the ground ribeye steak patty on top of the prime rib patty
> Use the SEAL side of the Burger Press to keep the two patties in place. Close the press firmly, which will seal the patties together. Release the press.
> Put the patties on the grill and cook for 6 minutes on each side.
> Serve on the onion bun and top with horseradish

Sweet BBQ Brisket and Bratwurst Burger

BBQ season is here and you are grilling up a storm, but what to do with all of these leftovers? Ground them and make burgers. Brisket and bratwurst both seem to be the belles of the ball when it comes to BBW and in this recipe, we will make sure that they still reign supreme.

Prep Time: 5 Minutes
Cook Time: 20 Minutes
Servings: 4

INGREDIENTS:
1 pound ground brisket
1 pound ground bratwurst
Kosher Salt
Fresh Ground Pepper
½ cup BBQ sauce
2 full tomatoes
4 hoagie rolls

DIRECTIONS:
> Mix the ground brisket and the ground bratwurst with the salt and people
> Form the ground brisket mixture and ground bratwurst mixture into eight 4 ounce balls. Create each ball into a patty by using the STUFF side of the burger press to push it down.
> Fill 1 of the brisket patties with half of the tomato.
> Place the ground bratwurst patty on top of the ground brisket patty
> Use the SEAL side of the Burger Press to keep the two patties in place. Close the press firmly, which will seal the patties together. Release the press.
> Put the patties on the grill and cook for 6 minutes on each side.
> Serve on the hoagie roll and top with the BBQ sauce.

Ground Chicken and Shrimp Burger

Chicken and shrimp have had a long standing relationship and we didn't feel that it was right to separate them. So, in this recipe we have decided to marry them in burger goodness. Please enjoy the reception.

Prep Time: 5 Minutes
Cook Time: 20 Minutes
Servings: 4

INGREDIENTS:

1 pound of ground chicken
1 pound of ground shrimp
Kosher Salt
Fresh Ground Pepper
½ cup of garbanzo beans
½ cup of tartar sauce
½ cup of lemon juice
8 servings of hamburger buns

DIRECTIONS:

> Mix the ground chicken and ground shrimp with the salt and pepper and lemon juice
> Form the ground chicken mixture and the ground shrimp mixture into eight 4 ounce balls. Create each ball into a patty by using the STUFF side of the burger press to push it down.
> Fill 1 of the chicken patties with a quarter of the garbanzo beans.
> Place the black bean patty on top of the other patty
> Use the SEAL side of the Burger Press to keep the two patties in place. Close the press firmly, which will seal the patties together. Release the press.
> Put the patties on the grill and cook for 6 minutes on each side.
> Serve on the hamburger bun and top with tartar sauce.

Chorizo and Black Bean Burger

In this recipe we have decided to introduce pork chorizo to the black bean burger. By combining the two, you will feel like you are having a whole Mexican style dinner in every bite. Don't forget to add some Mexican Rice to complete the meal.

Prep Time: 5 Minutes
Cook Time: 20 Minutes
Servings: 4

INGREDIENTS:

1 pound pork chorizo sausage
1 can of black beans
Kosher Salt
Fresh Ground Pepper
4 habanero's
¼ cup of Tabasco sauce
8 servings of hamburger buns

DIRECTIONS:

> Mix the ground pork sausage with the salt and pepper
> Drain the can of black beans and mash them up
> Form the ground sausage mixture and the black bean mixture into eight 4 ounce balls. Create each ball into a patty by using the STUFF side of the burger press to push it down.
> Fill 1 of the 4 patties with 1 habanero.
> Place the black bean patty on top of the pork sausage patty
> Use the SEAL side of the Burger Press to keep the two patties in place. Close the press firmly, which will seal the patties together. Release the press.
> Put the patties on the grill and cook for 6 minutes on each side.
> Serve on the bun with Tabasco sauce

Ground Bacon and Beef Burger

French Fries and Hamburgers are like Macaroni and Cheese, Peanut Butter and Jelly. They are a pair that is so good together; they are sold in every chain across the country. Well, in this recipe we took it to a whole 'nother level. Here we add the French fries inside the burger. Bamn!

Prep Time: 5 Minutes
Cook Time: 20 Minutes
Servings: 4

INGREDIENTS:
1 pound ground beef
1 pound ground bacon
Kosher Salt
Fresh Ground Pepper
½ cup French fries
1 tsp. garlic pepper
8 servings of sourdough buns, split and toasted

DIRECTIONS:
> Mix the ground beef and bacon with salt and pepper separately
> Form the ground beef mixture and ground bacon into four 4 ounce balls. Create each ball into a patty by using the STUFF side of the burger press to push it down.
> Top 1 of the beef patties with a quarter of the French fries.
> Place one ground bacon patty on top of the ground beef patty
> Use the SEAL side of the Burger Press to keep the two patties in place. Close the press firmly, which will seal the patties together. Release the press.
> Put the patties on the grill and cook for 6 minutes on each side.
> Serve on the sourdough and top with ketchup, yellow mustard and onion slices.

FRUIT STUFFED BURGERS:

Stuffed Cinnamon Apple Chicken Burger

Fruit can do so much to a dish. Here we stuff the ground chicken with tart granny smith apples and rub cinnamon all over it. We want to give your taste buds a different experience.

Prep Time: 5 Minutes
Cook Time: 20 Minutes
Servings: 4

INGREDIENTS:

1½ lbs. lean ground chicken sausage
Kosher Salt
Fresh Ground Pepper
½ cup cinnamon
2 full granny smith apples, de-seeded
8 servings of hamburger buns

DIRECTIONS:

> Mix the ground chicken with the ground cinnamon
> Form the ground chicken mixture into eight 4 ounce balls. Create each ball into a patty by using the STUFF side of the burger press to push it down.
> Fill 1 of the patties with half of the apple.
> Place the other patty on top of the other patty
> Use the SEAL side of the Burger Press to keep the two patties in place. Close the press firmly, which will seal the patties together. Release the press.
> Put the patties on the grill and cook for 6 minutes on each side.
> Serve on the bun and top with some applesauce.

Sliced Orange Pork Burger

Description: Oranges are a great snack on a warm spring or summer day. Their juiciness really can fix your sweet cravings. In this recipe, the sweet juice of the orange is cooked right into the burger for a sweet taste that will you will love.

Prep Time: 5 Minutes
Cook Time: 20 Minutes
Servings: 4

INGREDIENTS:

1 ½ ground pork
4 oranges, peeled and sliced
½ cup rosemary
1 carrot, shaved
1 cup of red cabbage
1 cub Napa cabbage
½ cup mayonnaise
½ cup lemon juice
Salt and pepper
4 hamburger bans, split

> Directions:
> Combine the ground pork, rosemary and lemon juice
> Combine the carrots, mayonnaise, and cabbage together to make a salad
> Form the ground pork into eight 4 ounce balls. Create each ball into a patty by using the STUFF side of the burger press to push it down.
> Fill 1 of the patties with one full orange.
> Place the other patty on top of the other patty
> Use the SEAL side of the Burger Press to keep the two patties in place. Close the press firmly, which will seal the patties together. Release the press.
> Put the patties on the grill and cook for 6 minutes on each side
> Place the burgers on top of a bun and top with the salad mixture.

Stuffed Banana Ground Beef Burger

The sweetness of the banana is great with almost anything. This is why we are adding it in this burger in place of the French fries.

Prep Time: 5 Minutes
Cook Time: 20 Minutes
Servings: 4

INGREDIENTS:

1½ lbs. lean ground beef
Kosher Salt
Fresh Ground Pepper
½ cup of peanut butter
1 full banana, sliced
8 servings of hamburger buns

DIRECTIONS:

> Mix the ground beef with the salt and pepper
> Form the ground beef mixture into eight 4 ounce balls. Create each ball into a patty by using the STUFF side of the burger press to push it down.
> Fill 1 of the patties with half of the 2 slices of the banana.
> Place the other patty on top of the other patty
> Use the SEAL side of the Burger Press to keep the two patties in place. Close the press firmly, which will seal the patties together. Release the press.
> Put the patties on the grill and cook for 6 minutes on each side.
> Serve on the bun and top with some peanut butter

Stuffed Pears Turkey Burger

Pears are a very crisp, sweet and juicy fruit. They will pair well with the ground turkey and mix well in the meat. The sweetness along with the nuttiness of the gorgonzola is a culinary success.

Prep Time: 5 Minutes
Cook Time: 20 Minutes
Servings: 4

INGREDIENTS:
1½ lbs. ground turkey
Kosher Salt
Fresh Ground Pepper
½ cup gorgonzola
2 full pears, split and de-seeded
8 servings of hamburger buns

DIRECTIONS:
> Mix the ground turkey with the salt and pepper
> Form the ground turkey mixture into eight 4 ounce balls. Create each ball into a patty by using the STUFF side of the burger press to push it down.
> Fill 1 of the patties with half of the pear.
> Place the other patty on top of the other patty
> Use the SEAL side of the Burger Press to keep the two patties in place. Close the press firmly, which will seal the patties together. Release the press.
> Put the patties on the grill and cook for 6 minutes on each side.
> Serve: on the bun and top with condiments of your choice.

Bing Cherry Stuffed Burger

Cherries are a very tart fruit and this tartness will add a new element to the ground beef. The sweet and sour flavor makes it so that you don't have to marinate the meat in anything else.

Prep Time: 5 Minutes
Cook Time: 20 Minutes
Servings: 4

INGREDIENTS:
1½ lbs. lean ground beef
Kosher Salt
Fresh Ground Pepper
8 full Bing cherries, de-pitted
8 servings of hamburger buns

DIRECTIONS:
> Mix the ground beef with the salt and pepper
> Form the ground beef mixture into eight 4 ounce balls. Create each ball into a patty by using the STUFF side of the burger press to push it down.
> Fill 1 of the patties with 2 full cherries.
> Place the other patty on top of the other patty
> Use the SEAL side of the Burger Press to keep the two patties in place. Close the press firmly, which will seal the patties together. Release the press.
> Put the patties on the grill and cook for 6 minutes on each side.
> Serve: on the bun and top with any condiments of your choice.

Watermelon Stuffed Ground Rib Burger

Ribs and watermelon are a great combination during BBQ's. Here we decided to make a burger out of them. It'll blow your mind. Just don't forget to buy seedless.

Prep Time: 5 Minutes
Cook Time: 20 Minutes
Servings: 4

INGREDIENTS:

1½ lbs. ground beef rib meat
Kosher Salt
Fresh Ground Pepper
½ cup BBQ sauce
4 slices of watermelon, seedless
8 servings of sesame hamburger buns

DIRECTIONS:

> Mix the ground rib meat with the salt, pepper and BBQ sauce
> Form the ground rib mixture into eight 4 ounce balls. Create each ball into a patty by using the STUFF side of the burger press to push it down.
> Fill 1 of the patties with one watermelon slice.
> Place the other patty on top of the other patty
> Use the SEAL side of the Burger Press to keep the two patties in place. Close the press firmly, which will seal the patties together. Release the press.
> Put the patties on the grill and cook for 6 minutes on each side.
> Serve on the bun with the leftover BBQ sauce.

Papaya Stuffed Spam Burger

Papaya is often compared to coffee because it is an acquired taste. Today we will make you a believer. This papaya stuffed spam burger will remind you of the islands. Feel free to eat it with rice if you like.

Prep Time: 5 Minutes
Cook Time: 20 Minutes
Servings: 4

INGREDIENTS:

1½ lbs. ground spam
Kosher Salt
Fresh Ground Pepper
½ cup of salsa
1 full papaya cut in quarters
8 servings of hamburger buns

DIRECTIONS:

›   Mix the ground spam with the salt and pepper
›   Form the ground spam mixture into eight 4 ounce balls. Create each ball into a patty by using the STUFF side of the burger press to push it down.
›   Fill 1 of the patties with a quarter of the papaya
›   Place the other patty on top of the other patty
›   Use the SEAL side of the Burger Press to keep the two patties in place. Close the press firmly, which will seal the patties together. Release the press.
›   Put the patties on the grill and cook for 6 minutes on each side.
›   Serve on the bun and top with some of the salsa.

Strawberry Stuffed Sausage Patty Breakfast Burger

What better way to pay a tribute to the breakfast sausage then to stuff it with strawberries and top it with cream or even maple syrup. Either way, this is your breakfast burger.

Prep Time: 5 Minutes
Cook Time: 20 Minutes
Servings: 4

INGREDIENTS:

1 ½ ground sausage
Kosher Salt
Fresh Ground Pepper
2 large strawberries cut in half and top cut off
4 biscuits, split and toasted

DIRECTIONS:

> Mix the ground sausage with the salt and pepper
> Form the ground sausage mixture into eight 4 ounce balls. Create each ball into a patty by using the STUFF side of the burger press to push it down.
> Fill 1 of the patties with half of the strawberry
> Place the other patty on top of the other patty
> Use the SEAL side of the Burger Press to keep the two patties in place. Close the press firmly, which will seal the patties together. Release the press.
> Put the patties on the grill and cook for 6 minutes on each side.
> Serve on the biscuit with butter, honey or jelly.

Cheesy Scrambled Eggs Ground Bacon Burgers

This burger is the whole breakfast experience, but where the bacon is the star. That's okay; eggs take it all the time anyway. Here the cheesy scrambled eggs are second to the bacon. That's okay, it tastes good either way.

Prep Time: 5 Minutes
Cook Time: 20 Minutes
Servings: 4

INGREDIENTS:

1½ lbs. ground bacon
Kosher Salt
Fresh Ground Pepper
2 scrambled eggs
½ shredded cheddar cheese
4 English Muffins, toasted and split
Strawberry or grape jelly for tasting

DIRECTIONS:

> Scramble the eggs to there are done and add the cheese until it melts. Set aside.
> Mix the ground bacon with salt and pepper
> Form the ground bacon mixture into eight 4 ounce balls. Create each ball into a patty by using the STUFF side of the burger press to push it down.
> Fill 1 of the patties with a quarter of the scrambled egg mix.
> Place the other patty on top of the other patty
> Use the SEAL side of the Burger Press to keep the two patties in place. Close the press firmly, which will seal the patties together. Release the press.
> Put the patties on the grill and cook for 6 minutes on each side.
> Serve on the English Muffins and top with ketchup, strawberry or grape jam.

"BONUS" Chapter 10: "BONUS" MARINADES!

10 HAND SELECTED MOUTHWATERING MARINADES FOR MEATS:

Always remember..."Marinade that meat people!" If you want your meat to be an amazingly "High Flavored, Smack in the Mouth" taste that you've never experienced before...then we have "**this bonus section**" for you! These are our 10 favorite marinades that we pulled out of "Our Play Book" just for you! Every pulsating taste of bliss that you'll every want on your meat is right here at your fingertips!

Someone once asked me if I marinade my meats! My response was..."ABSOLUTELY!" This is a regular practice for me and I take pride in this process. My theory on this one is..."If you have a piece of meat, then it better be soaking in some delicious juices that will have you begging for more. Now...take your meal and "Dive in Head First" to these delicious meat soaking juices! ;)

APPLE CIDER HOT MUSTARD GARLIC MARINADE:

INGREDIENTS:

1/2 cup apple cider vinegar
1/2 cup dry mustard
4 tbsp. of garlic juice

1/3 cup sugar
1 egg
1 cup mayonnaise

DIRECTIONS:

> Combine all of these ingredients, except the garlic and mayonnaise, in a blender for best results!
> Prepare and warm up these ingredients in a pan on medium heat.
> You will start to see the sauce get thicker.
> After it thickens from the heat mix in 4 tbsp. of garlic juice 1 cup mayonnaise and stir the mixture!
> Now mix your meat up in that before cooking!

CINNAMON BASIL HONEY MARINADE WITH GARLIC

INGREDIENTS:

1/2 cup onion (minced)
1/4 cup fresh lemon juice
1/4 cup avocado oil
2 tbsp. low sodium soy sauce
2 cloves garlic (crushed or minced)

1 tbsp. ginger (grated fresh)
2 tbsp. honey
1/2 tsp. cinnamon
1 tsp. basil
2 tsp. chopped fresh parsley

DIRECTIONS:

> Combine all of these ingredients together in a blender for best results!

WHITE WINE JALAPEÑO/CAYENNE MARINADE

INSTRUCTIONS:

2 1/2 cups white wine (dry)
1/2 teaspoon cayenne pepper
1 jalapeno pepper (minced)
1 teaspoon onion powder

1/2 cup soy sauce
1/2 teaspoon garlic powder
1/2 tsp. parsley
1/2 tsp. fresh ground pepper

DIRECTIONS:

› Combine all of these ingredients together in a blender for best results!

RED WINE SWEET CAJUN MARINADE

INSTRUCTIONS:

1/3 cup soy sauce & 1/2 cup red wine
2 tablespoons Cajun seasoning
2 tablespoons minced garlic
2 tablespoons brown sugar

1/2 teaspoon cinnamon
1 tablespoon tomato paste
1 teaspoon freshly ground black pepper
1 splash of lemon juice

DIRECTIONS:

> Combine all of these ingredients together in a blender for best results!

LEMON PEPPER BASIL MARINADE

INGREDIENTS:

2/3 cup lemon juice

3 oz. water

2 teaspoons chicken bouillon (granules)

2 cloves garlic (minced)

1 teaspoon pepper (fresh ground)

1/2 teaspoon basil

DIRECTIONS:

> Combine all of these ingredients together in a blender for best results!

MOUTH WATERING MEXICAN STYLE MARINADE

INGREDIENTS:

1/4 cup lime juice
1/4 cup avocado oil
1/3 cup water
1 tablespoon vinegar
2 teaspoons soy sauce (low sodium)
2 teaspoons Worcestershire sauce
1 clove garlic, minced

1/2 teaspoon chili powder
1/2 teaspoon beef bouillon paste
1/2 teaspoon ground cumin
1/2 teaspoon cilantro
1/2 teaspoon dried oregano
1/4 teaspoon ground black pepper

DIRECTIONS:

› Combine all of these ingredients together in a blender for best results!

PINEAPPLE RASPBERRY MEAT TWISTER MARINADE

INGREDIENTS:

1/2 cup raspberry preserves
1/2 teaspoon lemon juice
1/2 cup pineapple juice
1/2 cup soy sauce

2 tablespoons rice vinegar
1/2 teaspoon minced garlic
1/2 teaspoon dried basil

DIRECTIONS:

> Combine all of these ingredients together in a blender for best results!

ITALIAN MEAT MARINATING MAGNIFIER

INGREDIENTS:

1/2 cup Italian dressing
1/2 teaspoon lemon juice
1/2 teaspoon minced garlic

1/2 teaspoon dried basil
1/2 teaspoon Tabasco sauce

DIRECTIONS:

> Combine all of these ingredients together in a blender for best results!

MILD MARINADE SEAFOOD SOAKER

INSTRUCTIONS:

1/2 cup onion (minced)
1/4 cup fresh lemon juice
1/8 cup avocado oil

1/8 cup butter (almond butter best)
2 tsp. chopped fresh parsley

DIRECTIONS:

> Combine all of these ingredients together in a blender for best results!

WHITE WINE SEAFOOD GARLIC MARINADE

INSTRUCTIONS:

2 1/2 cups white wine (dry)
1/8 cup avocado oil
1 tbsp. Old Bay Seasoning

1/4 cup fresh lemon juice
2 tsp. chopped parsley (fresh)
2 tsp. paprika

DIRECTIONS:

> Combine all of these ingredients together in a blender for best results!

DID YOU APPRECIATE THIS PUBLICATION? HERE'S WHAT YOU DO NOW...

If you were pleased with our book then you can **Go to Amazon where you purchased this book and <u>leave us a review</u>!** In the world of an author who writes books independently, your reviews are not only touching but important so that we know you like the material we have prepared for "YOU" our audience! So leave us a review...we would love to see that you enjoyed our book!

If for any reason that you were less than happy with your experience then send me an email at feedback@HealthyLifestyleRecipes.org and let me know how we can better your experience. We always come out with a few volumes of our books and will possibly be able to address some of your concerns. Do keep in mind that we strive to do our best to give you the highest quality of what "we the independent authors" pour our heart and tears into.

Again...I really appreciate your purchase and thank you for your many great reviews and comments! With a warm heart! ~Richard Erwin

A LITTLE ABOUT THE AUTHOR OF THIS BOOK

Richard Erwin is a trained, self taught, private gourmet chef (and burger expert) that has enjoyed his craft in the kitchens of many celebrities and exclusive events of Southern California and Texas. He enjoys creating new recipes for an array of categories and writes recipes and books from his heart and soul to share with you!

WANT FREE BOOKS?
... OF COURSE YOU DO!

OUR NEW BOOKS SENT TO YOUR EMAIL MONTHLY

For our current readers...if you like receiving FREE Books to add to your collection, then this is for you! This is for promoting our material to our current members so you can review our new books and give us feed back when we launch new books we are publishing! This helps us determine how we can make our books better for YOU, our audience! Just go to the url below and leave your name and email. We will send you a complimentary book about once a month. And just an FYI...on the website we've posted a few videos for you here too...

"Additional Marinades"
Yours FREE for signing up to Our List!

www.HealthyLifestyleRecipes.org/FreeBook2Review

Made in the USA
Middletown, DE
06 May 2018